COLORADO'S ECCENTRIC

CAPTAIN JACK

A reprint of
The Fate of a Fairy or
Twenty Seven Years in the Far West

by Ellen E. Jack

Lake City, Colorado

A Reprint Published by
Western Reflections Publishing Company
P. O. Box 1149
951 N. Highway 149
Lake City, CO 81235

www.westernreflectionspublishing.com

Cover Design by Angela Hollingsworth
APH creative design, Lake City, CO

Printed in the United States of America

ISBN 978-1-932738-89-6

PUBLISHER'S FOREWORD

Of all the women who migrated to Colorado during the great gold and silver mining years of the late nineteenth century, Ellen E. Jack was one of the most unusual, eccentric, and noteworthy. She was born in Nottingham, England on November 4, 1842, to William and Elizabeth Elliott. The Elliotts were well-to-do manufacturers of Nottingham lace and raised nine children on their large family estate.

Ellen always had a mystical nature about her, even as a young child. She later wrote that a gypsy told her as a seven-year-old that she "was born to be a great traveler, and if she had been a male would have been a great mining expert. She is a Rosicrucian, born to find hidden treasure. She will meet great sorrow and be a widow early in life." (Rosicrucians were a secret society in the seventeenth through nineteenth centuries that laid claim to various forms of occult knowledge and powers.)

Ellen was very intelligent and very good-looking, with light blond hair. During her youth, her family moved out of the home that had been in the family for over 300 years and went to Manchester, where her father lost most of their money in a failed brewery venture. As she grew into adulthood, Ellen had a Russian lover who was extremely jealous and stabbed her three times when he saw her at the opera with her male cousin.

Doctors prescribed a sea voyage for the ailing Ellen. She went to New York with her sister and brother-in-law, but her health took a turn for the worse, and she returned to England. On the return voyage she met her future husband, Charles E. Jack, who was the first officer on the ship. Before the voyage was over he had proposed, and on September 9, 1860, they were married in England. Shortly afterwards Charles was made captain of his own ship. Eighteen-year-old Ellen returned with her new husband to the United States and lived with his family when he was gone on voyages. Aristocratic Ellen was disappointed and offended by what she perceived to be the crude manner of dress and manners of the Americans.

Soon after Ellen arrived in the United States, the Civil War broke out. Her husband became a Captain in the Union Navy and was called "Captain Charles Jack" thereafter. While, his father, the owner of several ships, was known as "Colonel Jack." Ellen became part of Washington society during the war and met the Lincolns and many of the top Union generals and their wives. Captain Jack discovered a personal item belonging to General Robert E. Lee on a steamboat during the war. After the hostilities were over, he returned the item to Lee who gave him a diamond ring with the date 1314 inscribed on it. Lee also told Captain Jack of many mysterious adventures that surrounded the ring, which Charles gave to Ellen. At this time Ellen also received her share of what was left of the Elliott family fortune.

After the war, Ellen's husband and two of her three children died and a good part of her fortune, which had been invested in commercial buildings, was destroyed in fires. The gypsy's prophecy had been partially fulfilled. She wrote that she was insane with grief. Ellen set up a trust fund for her daughter, put her in boarding school, and moved to Pueblo and then Denver, Colorado, where she started using the name "Captain Jack" for herself. During this time she hung around with spiritualists and mediums and gained a reputation for curing the sick. One of her spiritualist friends verified that she thought Ellen was a Rosicrucian and would find a great treasure. It was at this time that she was first called a "fairy" – by a man who wanted her for his dance hall. Ellen had to fight off his advances with her two .44 pistols. She then moved to Gunnison, Colorado, where large deposits of gold had just been found. During the stage ride to Gunnison she carried the .44 revolvers and had her jewelry, bonds, and cash sewn into her bustle. An attempt was made to holdup the stage, but she and future Governor Alva Adams held off the bandits.

Exactly where Ellen went next is subject to debate. She later said that she established the tiny community of Jack's Cabin northwest of Gunnison. It was a rest stop for freighters traveling between Crested Butte and Gunnison, but only contained a few cabins at its peak time. Noted Colorado historian Muriel Wolle (*Stampede to Timberline*) credits Jack Howe with starting the community, which eventually gained a few more cabins, a school and a cemetery. Ellen writes in her book that she set up several boarding houses in Gunnison using the name "Jack's Cabin." Whether she founded the community of Jack's Cabin or not, Ellen bought controlling interest in several coal mines and the Black Queen Mine that was rich in silver and zinc. The mine was located about a mile north of the town of Crystal on the other side of the Elk Mountains and about half way between Crested Butte and Aspen. Captain Jack visited both Jack's Cabin and Crystal frequently for supplies.

In Gunnison, Ellen claimed to have witnessed many gunfights, had Indians try to buy her, and scorned many potential lovers (one of whom called her his "Fairy Queen"). Sometimes it is a little hard to tell fact from fiction in Ellen's writing, because the events in which she claimed to have taken part seem so unbelievable.

As Inez Hunt and Wanetta W. Draper wrote in their book, *To Colorado's Restless Ghosts*, "Ellen had thought for a long time that her life was controlled by spirits – that she had spirits all around her all the time, that good or evil, they influenced her." As a result she followed her first impressions in business transactions, assuming that the spirits were telling her what to do. If she waited, and thought matters over, she was sure that she would make the wrong decision. However, she did not pay heed to the spirits when she entered into her second marriage.

Ellen accepted the marriage proposal of a man named "Walsh" (she never gave his first name) who was twenty years older than her. Upon leaving for Denver to get married, she immediately began to feel that the spirits of her dead children and husband were telling her not to take this step. When she attempted to back out, Walsh called her a coward and she decided to go through with the ceremony. Her new husband left and never came back to their hotel that honeymoon night. It would take years for Ellen to obtain an annulment, get her mine released, and clear up her financial affairs; even though Walsh was already married at the time he "married" her.

After her problems had started with Walsh, Captain Jack spent much more time at her mine. She often ran it by herself and experienced avalanches, shootings, a mountain lion in her bed (it turned out to be someone's pet), a deadly "mountain fever epidemic," the threat of a Ute massacre, a gun battle between her and outlaws, and a physical fight in court between her and others.

Ellen was forced to sell her Gunnison property to obtain an annulment from Walsh. She sold the Black Queen Mine for $25,000 (a large sum in those days); but the mine sold one year later for $3,000,000! Ellen later contended that the mine was worth $42,000,000. During this same period, Captain Jack also obtained a scar on her forehead that she attributed to a poisoned Ute tomahawk during the "Gunnison Uprising." She carried the scar the rest of her life and was always quick to relate the story behind it. There is no record of such an uprising anywhere near Aspen or Gunnison, but Captain Jack did have the scar.

Ellen then went to Ouray, Colorado, where she supposedly discovered a rich silver mine on Bear Creek, and then she went to Utah and Nevada where she was also successful at prospecting. It is at this point that her book ends.

In 1900, Captain Jack settled near Colorado Springs on what was called the "High Drive," which overlooked the city. She "prospected" extensively in the area with a string of burros carrying her supplies, filed several mining claims, and built a cabin. She was sure that it was here that she would find the treasure that the gypsies had told her about; and it was during this time that she wrote *The Fate of a Fairy*, which was published in 1910. In her autobiography she reveals much of the unusual philosophy she formed during her life:

> There is a power far stronger than that which forces us to our destiny, and we ought to be on our guard all the time for strangers that we know not, for some people carry a straight light around them that is destructive to one that carries the opposite light. For when a murder wave or suicide wave comes to a city you will know there will be many before it travels on... There is a triangle of three powers that govern both heaven and earth – electricity, vibration, and this force power....

Captain Jack went on to write that the force came in different colors and performed differently depending on its color. She felt that not just individuals but nations were affected by these waves. She predicted that this power would make "airships" possible, that farmers would plow with it instead of using horses and mules, and that trains would be powered by it. In the meantime, she felt that the "waves" were playing havoc in the world by causing everything from drunkenness to earthquakes. She felt that she would be safer in the mountains of the West, so Captain Jack spent summers at her claims on the High Drive where she would give tours and talk to the tourists about mining, charge for rides on her burros, pose for pictures, sell her book, and tell tall tales to anyone who would listen. She had several little cabins that she rented out. Many a tour from Colorado Springs ended at Captain Jack's place in the mountains. A horseback trail led directly from the Broadmoor Hotel to

Captain Jack's Cabin. It was indeed a beautiful place in the pines overlooking "The Springs," and Captain Jack was a colorful figure from a time gone by.

In the winter, Captain Jack moved into her small house in Colorado Springs. True to her unusual ways she often had her brightly colored parrots in the trees in front of her house. In the spring of 1921, Captain Jack wasn't feeling well but desperately wanted to go back to her High Drive property. However extreme spring floods washed out the road and made the drive impossible. Captain Jack died in Colorado Springs on June 17, 1921. She was seventy-eight years old. She was buried in the Evergreen Cemetery, close to General Palmer, founder of Colorado Springs. A fitting epitaph might well be "She lived a very unusual and different life."

ACKNOWLEDGEMENT

Many thanks to Henry Woods, who furnished the original copy of this work to Western Reflections Publishing Company

Mrs. Capt. Jack Looking for a Company to Buy Mine, 1907.

THE

FATE OF A FAIRY

BY

ELLEN E. JACK

CHICAGO
M. A. DONOHUE & CO.
PUBLISHERS

ILLUSTRATIONS

FACING PAGE

THE FATE OF A FAIRY

CHAPTER I.

I WAS born November 4, 1842, in New Lentern, Nottingham, England, my parents being William and Elizabeth Elliott. My father was one of the patentees and manufacturers of the famous Nottingham lace curtains. We belonged to the Quaker sect, and the house I was born in was the original Fox homestead, it having been occupied in continuous time for over three hundred years. I had five brothers—William, Charles, Isaac, Henry and Frank—who all entered the British navy as midshipmen, afterward becoming officers of higher rank. I had also three sisters—Eliza, Lydia and Betsy Ann. My sister Betsy Ann was burned to death when very young, and my sister Lydia got married, I going to live with her afterward.

One chilly evening in the beginning of November, in the year 1849, I stood, a little fair-haired girl dressed in the English style of low-necked dress with short sleeves, looking at a string of covered wagons belonging to a tribe of gypsies that were looking for a place to camp. It was the time of the Goose Fair at Nottingham, which is a beautiful, thrifty and prosperous manufacturing town of England. The law was very strict, it being imprisonment or fine if gypsies were found camping on the highway or on city property. They were trying to see if they could get permission to occupy one of the fields, and as they caught sight of me watching them, they spoke in their own language. Then the queen, a tall, dark woman, came over to me and said:

"Who lives in that house among the trees?"

I said, "My mamma."

"Well, you are the fairest little one I have ever seen. Come and take me to your mamma."

So she took my hand and we both went to my mother, and the queen told her she would pay her well for the use of the ground while the fair lasted and that not a blade of grass should be harmed by her tribe if she would let them in. My mother said, "They say gypsies steal children. Would thee steal mine?"

The queen said: "I give thee my hand and pledge that we will not steal anything belonging to you, or let anyone else, if we know it."

So she gave five pounds to my mother, then she turned my hair back from my forehead and said:

"This child was born to be a great traveler, and if she had been a male would have been a great mining expert. She is a Rosicrusian, born to find hidden treasures. She will meet great sorrows and be a widow early in life. Fire will cause her great trouble and losses."

My mother did not believe in fortune-telling and paid no attention to the predictions of the queen. After that the gates were opened and the tribe came in. It was getting cold and dark, but I wanted to see what they were going to do, so I stole away to watch them at their work. Some were putting up the tents, others were making camp-fires; all was life and everyone knew what to do. When the work was done they all gathered around the fire and sang and played fiddles, tambourines and other instruments of which I do not know the names. I could not understand a word that was said, and that puzzled me very much. It was a strange sight to see such a merry lot of dark-looking people outside the tents and around the big fire. We afterward learned that they were the Boswell tribe, and that the men were veterinary doctors and horse-traders and the women made fancy baskets and told fortunes.

The queen had a grand-daughter a year older than I, whose name was Zephey. She was a marvel for one so young. She could dance and sing, play the tambourine and castanets, and with bones between her fingers would keep time to her dancing. She was very pretty and it was a treat to see her at her antics. A great attachment sprang up between her and me, and she tried to teach me her songs and told me many things about the tribe.

It was now getting toward the close of the fair, and on Saturday the queen got Zephey and me to go with her to the walnut grove and get a great collection of husks. I soon found out what they were used for. They put them in a large pot of cold water, which they hung over the fire to get the color out. With this they dyed their hair, then diluted some with water and put it on their faces, necks and arms. This made their black hair as glossy as silk and gave them a clear, olive complexion. They fixed themselves up in this way on Saturday night and on Sunday morning went in a body to the church. The men had knee-breeches and buckles on their shoes, the old men wearing black stockings and the young men red ones. Black hats with red bands around, and shirts with turned-down rolling Byron collars, some with red handkerchiefs and some with black for ties, completed their picturesque costume. The women wore black beaver bonnets with long white plumes, and long scarlet cloaks with yokes that covered their dresses. They walked in pairs to the church and took seats together in one corner. After the service two of the young people were married. It was a gypsy wedding conducted according to the laws of England, but they had another form which they went through after they got back to their tents.

They all came outside and formed a circle around the bride and groom. The queen had a gold charm in a piece of black velvet hanging in the center of her forehead, which she always wore. She had on a white dress with wide, flowing sleeves. Zephey carried a wreath and bouquet of everlasting daisy flowers. They stood in the center of the circle. Then the queen threw up her left sleeve and above the elbow was a bracelet in the form of a serpent, all a-glitter with diamonds and rubies. She then took a penknife concealed within the bracelet and going over to the groom cut a small hole in his shirt, right over his heart. Into this she put the bouquet and then placed the wreath on the bride's head, saying:

"The fresh, beautiful flowers that bloom with their fragrance in the sun soon droop and perish, the slightest frost withers them, but I crown you with the everlasting daisies, which storm nor frost cannot destroy. My children, may your lives be as simple and your love for each other as everlasting as these simple wild flowers."

Then the songs started and all kinds of merriment and feasting were indulged in until a late hour.

The next morning at sunrise they took down their tents, packed up and went away and I saw no more of them for two years.

My great-grandmother was 107 years old and very childish. People would come for miles around to see the old granny who lived in the old homestead originally the home of George Fox, from whom our family was descended. My grandmother's maiden name was Mary Fox and her mother was of the same name, all born in this homestead, which consisted of beautiful grounds that surrounded the quaint old thatched cottage. It stood on the bank of the river Trent, and the famous regattas could be seen from the bank near the house. The house was buried amid the old oak trees and the sides were covered with creeping ivy and clinging moss roses. The roof was covered with mosses of different colors and a more romantic and beautiful place could not be found. Clifton Grove, which was a great pleasure resort, was one-half mile from us, and Willford, our little village, was one mile from Nottingham.

Granny knew that I attracted as much attention for being a very smart and attractive child as she did for her great age and ancient appearance, and in consequence took a great dislike to me. If she could find me alone she would beat me unmercifully and tear my hair out by the handful. In fact she became so vicious that mother had to keep a constant watch on me for fear she would kill me.

I would go out rambling in the fields and hills when my mother would be absent, singing to myself and filling my apron with blackberries, primroses and wildflowers. While on one of these excursions to the hills I thought of what the gypsy queen had told me, that I was born to find hidden treasure, so I procured a knife and went down to the bank of the river Trent and began to dig, thinking this was the bank my father had spoken of when he said he had put his money in the bank, but all I got for my trouble was to have the folk laugh at me.

About a month later granny sat watching a winding sheet in the candle and said she would not go to bed until she found out if it was a young or old person who was going to die. She said it was a sure token of early death if the winding sheet dropped off before the candle was much burned; if it stayed on until the candle was burned out it would be an old person; if it dropped in the middle it would be a person of middle age. So she watched the candle until it was burned out and then said:

"I will go to bed now, for I have found out that I will soon leave this place and will meet William, my husband."

At 10 o'clock the next morning she was dead. Then I could go about withcut having my hair torn out.

Two years have passed and Nottingham Goose Fair is close at hand. I have not seen aught of the gypsies, but I had a presentiment that they would come this year, so I began to gather dry leaves, as the fair is held in November and the leaves were falling. I gathered a large bed of them and was as busy as a bee, gathering sticks for their fires, so that when they came they would have them at hand. I did not work in vain, for two days before the fair the gypsies came and I got hugged by the whole party, old and young, for the trouble I had been to in preparing for their reception. I was surprised to find how beautiful Zephey, the 10-year old gypsy girl, had grown. She asked me if I remembered the songs she had taught me when she was there before, but I was too young to recollect. The queen brought me a tambourine for a present, which delighted me very much, and I soon began to sing the gypsy girls' songs.

There was a horse disease, like the glanders, raging at the time, but known at the present time as the epizootic, and the gypsy king, Boswell, being a veterinary surgeon, made plenty of money doctoring horses.

The gypsies were making preparations to depart when the little girl Zephey took sick and died. I was so much attached to her that they could not persuade me to leave her until the funeral, which was indeed a very sad affair. Eight young gypsy women dressed in white, with white silk hoods and white scarfs, crossed over the right shoulder and tied with black ribbon under the left arm, were the pallbearers. Two went first, two on each side and two behind, carrying the coffin, and when halfway to the church they changed places. The two that were in the front and the two behind took the places of the four that had been carrying the coffin, and the latter fell into the places of the four that had relieved them. All the band of gypsies followed by twos, the Women wearing long scarlet cloaks and large black beaver bonnets with long white plumes.

When they got to the grave in the churchyard, they all knelt around the grave and began to chant in their own dialect, which I could not understand. I stood at a short distance watching them with tears coursing down my cheeks. After they had performed their strange burial rites, I remained and gathered my apron full of wild flowers, which I strewed over Zephey's grave. Then I sat down and sang:

"Death has been here and borne away
A sister from our side,
Just in the morning of her day,
As young as me she died.

"Not long ago she filled her place,
And sat with us to learn,
And now she's run her mortal race,
Which never can return."

It was sad for me so young, sitting all alone in the twilight, as darkness came and I looked at the last resting place of one I loved as a sister. I had never seen death before and it seemed as though I could not have so beautiful a girl as Zephey was left all alone in the ground with darkness coming on. I dried my eyes, however, and went home with a very heavy heart, but could not sleep until near morning. When nurse came to my bed I was in a raging fever. I had scarlet fever and was in a dangerous condition.

When the gypsies learned that I had caught the fever from Zephey they were very sorry and insisted that I was too young and fair for this world and that I would follow Zephey. In my ravings I would be singing the burial hymn and be gathering wild flowers for Zephey's grave. I was sick for many weeks and knew nothing, and when I came to my senses again the gypsies were all gone.

The next spring my parents left the old homestead which had been the home of my ancestors for over 300 years. My father bought the Albion brewery in Manchester and we moved there. The business was a failure, however, and we lost a lot of money.

One of my sisters got married to a wealthy merchant, and shortly after her marriage my father took sick with cholera. Every one of our neighbors became frightened for fear of contagion and left mother all alone. When I came home from school I found my father in great agony and nobody there to care for him but mother, so I went to the bed to rub him and do all I could to relieve his sufferings, but at 6 o'clock the same day he died.

Shortly after the death of my father my mother went back to New Lentern, near Nottingham, to live and I was left with my married sister. They owned a large house which no one would live in for ten years, as it had the reputation of being haunted. Her husband had it all newly painted and furnished, so we went to live there. The first night we were there all the bells in the house began to ring and we all got out of bed to see what was the matter. We made a search, but found nothing, and the servant girl left the next morning, saying the devil was in the house. My sister was very much frightened and her husband was puzzled.

The next night it was worse, if anything, than the former, for the bells rang so that we could not get any sleep. My sister would not stay in the house and left the fourth day, but I was anxious to see a ghost and remained to satisfy my curiosity. I slept all day and at night lit a rush-light candle and sat waiting for Mr. Ghost to make his music. I sat a long time before I heard or saw anything, but began to think we would have no concert that night, and was just about to go to bed when the bells began to ring.

I was sitting at the head of the stairs looking up to the bell wires, which were all in a row in the hall, when I saw the ghosts, a whole drove of rats, running back and forth over the wires. Their weight on the wires running back and forth caused the bells to ring. My sister came back the next day and when she found out the cause of the ringing she felt ashamed. Her husband put dogs and ferrets to work and soon got rid of the rats.

In a week or so after I had solved the great mystery of the haunted house my sister gave a party, to which she invited many nabobs, among them being a German family who brought with them a young gentleman, a Russian, who had come to England to finish his education. He was a very fine musician, a handsome man and highly educated, his large brown eyes having a dreamy expression. He went by the name of Carl, and when he sang and played my gypsy songs he made himself a great favorite with the company. After that night he came often to spend the evenings at my sister's and she began to joke about it and said I had a beau.

I thought so myself, but would not acknowledge the corn. Things went on smoothly for months and we took long rambles together, afoot, on horseback and in carriages, and he would call me his fairy. I thought him the finest man in the world, and with him I was the happiest creature on earth, but without him the world was a blank. We would sit on the bank of the river and I would play the guitar and sing, "Ever of thee I am fondly dreaming," while he would be all attention and throw pebbles into the brook.

When I had finished my song he took my hands in his and declared he could and would not live without me. He asked me to become his wife as soon as he had finished his studies, and so we became engaged. He called me his darling, I called him my beauty, and thought this world was fairer than ever before.

But alas! How soon was my air castle doomed

to fall and I doomed to disappointment! My foreign lover was called back to Russia to do military service, which was the custom of the country. After he had been gone three weeks my cousin, a young man by the name of Jack Dickson, came to the house and one evening asked me to go to the opera house to hear Piccolominni sing. I did not care to go, as I was grieving over the absence of my lover, but my sister begged me to go, so I went. I felt very sad all evening and paid no attention to the prima donna, as my thoughts were far away at that time. When we left the opera house I felt faint and caught hold of Cousin Jack. He went to buy a bouquet of flowers, and as I stood on the sidewalk waiting for him I was struck in the bosom three times with a dagger, the blade entering just above my heart. Jack came running to see what was the matter and was met by Carl, my Russian lover, who said that he would kill him if he put a hand on me, as he would rather see me dead than another man's wife. I fainted from loss of blood and at the same time the officers came, disarmed him and took him to prison.

I was put into a cab and driven home. When my wounds were dressed it was found that the first wound was one and one-half inches above my heart and the second about four inches to the right, both deep and painful and very dangerous. I was confined to my room for eighteen weeks and suffered much, but the pain in my poor tortured heart was worse than all. I thought it impossible that the hand that had held mine so confidently could in so brief a period strike me such a dreadful blow, and I wept many bitter tears and prayed God to forgive him, for he must surely have been mad with jealousy. I grew convalescent, but very slowly, and will carry the cruel scars to my grave.

Carl was released on payment of a big sum of money, but I was afraid of him. He begged to come and see me, but my sister stood firm and refused to let him enter the house.

My sister and her husband concluded to go to New York and began making preparations for the journey, as the firm with which he was connected had a branch there. I begged to go with them and they decided to take me along, as I was still very weak and the doctor said that it would be a great benefit for me to make the change.

On November 2, 1859, we left Liverpool in the "Harvest Queen" of the Black Ball Line, and on the voyage we were very sick for several days. Then we began to feel better and were able to come on deck. I was surprised to see so many women and children on the lower deck, going to their meals, and when we got on the coast of Ireland they took on a great many more passengers. The weather was very fine and we had no trouble in getting out of the channel, but after two days' sail from Holyhead a dreadful storm set in and everything was in confusion. The waves met together under the ship and it felt as though a cannon ball had struck it. The captain ordered all fires out as the storm increased. The steward brought us some cold meat and bread and cheese, as it was impossible to set the table, and this we ate from our hands. The steward was a colored man, and as he was handing some bread to a lady passenger the ship gave a plunge so suddenly that we all lost our balance and went sprawling on the floor. The steward tried to catch the table to save himself, but missed his hold and went over the table head foremost, hitting an old lady who was screaming at the top of her voice for God to help and save her.

I, being young, soon extricated myself from the mass and tried to help the rest, but when I saw the black man rolling among the ladies and heard their cries for help, the scene looked so ridiculous that instead of trying to help them I could do nothing for laughter. Such a sight I never shall forget. The noise of the waves, the wailing of the wind and the shrieks of the women, who were all piled together, was a scene not to be forgotten.

No one thought of undressing or going to bed that night, for our berths were all wet from the waves which came in through the portholes, so we made ourselves as comfortable as we could. In the morning I went up to the state cabin and put my head out of the scuttle, and what a sight met my eyes! The ship looked as if it were in a deep hole between the large waves of pale green water capped with white foam. The next moment with a bound it was on top of the waves and we shipped a big sea. The water nearly washed me off my feet and I was forced to go below and change my drenched clothing.

After the storm had abated and the men began to get things in order it was found that a young Irish girl in trying to get on deck had been washed by the waves against one of the hatches, breaking both of her legs. The doctor came into the cabin and said he wanted help, as the ship was rolling so badly that it was almost as much as he could do to steady himself. The ladies all declared that they could not go into steerage and bear the sight of the operation. I asked the doctor if I could be of any service to him and he said that I was rather young, but might as well learn young as any other time, so I went with him. He took a long rope and tied the unfortunate girl tightly so that she could not move nor roll around in her berth. He then went to work to set her limbs, but finding that this could not be done, decided that they must be amputated. He bound them up and left her until it would grow calm, so that the operation might be possible. She was a beautiful girl, eighteen years old, with large dark eyes and splendid white teeth.

It was a sad sight to see one so young and beautiful with so much affliction brought upon her in so brief a space of time, and I could not bring myself to realize her condition. I left her, telling her I would return in a few hours. It grew calmer and we all went to bed for the first time in two nights.

When I awoke the next morning, the sea was calm and the weather very fine. After breakfast I went to the steward's pantry and got some nice things to take to the sick girl, in company with the doctor, who went to see his patient. I gave her the breakfast and she ate heartily, saying that she was very hungry. When she had finished, the doctor commenced operating on her limbs. He took a mallet and a chisel and unjointed her limbs at the knees, and of all the horrible sounds that I have ever heard, that was the worst. The poor creature looked so pitifully at me with her large dark eyes while I held her hand, that I could scarcely keep from breaking down and I turned my back on the doctor, as I could not bear to witness the cruel operation.

The girl was pale as death and at times her eyes would glaze and she would cry: "Oh! mother, save me, save me!"

There were her brother and two cousins on board who knew that her limbs were being amputated, but they were on deck, reading their prayers out of their old Catholic prayer book. When the operation was over I did all that I could to sooth her, going every day to take her food from the cabin.

She told me that her unnatural father had turned her out of his house, and a sister in New York had sent her money enough to bring herself and brother out. It was a very sad meeting for those sisters. The young girl was engaged to a young blacksmith, who was a Protestant, and this was the cause of the trouble with her father, who had told her that if she did not break her engagement he would put her out of his house. This she refused to do and one night he turned her out into the cold, with neither bonnet nor shawl to protect her from the weather. I sang for her the verse of a song which ran as follows:

"Oh! cruel was that father, who shut his doors on me,
And cruel was the mother that such a sight could see,
And cruel were the bitter winds, that brought this grief on me."

When we came in sight of New York it presented the most beautiful sight I ever saw. I think it is the most beautiful harbor in the world and the clear blue sky was more beautiful than anything I had ever seen in England, where the sky looks smoky always. I was so delighted with the scenery, the banks of the Hudson, the views of Staten Island and the beautiful surroundings, that I felt I was in paradise.

We got to New York about 2 o'clock in the afternoon. I was taken to the Astor House on Broadway, and as I began to look around there was a big show on the corner of Fulton street. Across the way was the Astor House and Barnum's museum with its big pictures and a band on the outside. They were just starting another big hotel on Fourteenth and Broadway to be named the Fifth Avenue Hotel. I was there six weeks when I was taken ill with jaundice and became as yellow as a dandelion. By this time my brother-in-law had finished his business and was ready to return, but my condition was such that it was impossible for me to leave. They had secured a very good middle-aged woman to take care of me and I had a good old doctor, and as they could be of no further assistance I said, "Both of you go and I will come when I get better."

CHAPTER II.

THE winter was very lonely for me, a stranger in a foreign country and sick, so I got the nurse to look out for a good chance to go back. In March, 1860, we took passage on the "James Foster" of the Black Ball line, as the captain's wife and child were going on the voyage. At that time there were only two lines of steamers, the Cunard and the Inman, and they had only a few ships. It was a very cold morning when the carriage took me to the ship. I could not get up the plank, and the coachman was trying to help me when the first officer came forward, picked me up in his arms as though I was a child, and took me into the cabin and placed me on the lounge. He then called the stewardess to take my wraps and myself to the stateroom.

The captain's wife came and said: "You are the sick lady that is going with us?" I replied: "I am a canary bird now," for I was yellow with jaundice, "but I hope to get whiter and better by this voyage."

She went up on deck and told the captain and the mate that she had been to see me and she did not know which was the more yellow, my hair or my skin, and still I was so full of jokes and fun. The first officer then said:

"You will be surprised when I tell you that before this year is out that yellow girl will be my wife. When I saw her beautiful golden locks

I was attracted to her and when I picked her up in my arms I knew she belonged to me, and I will have her, let the weather be fair or foul."

The captain went and laid his hands on his shoulders and said:

"Yes, my boy, we salts can love and feel it deep down in our souls. Few land-lovers know the depth of feeling of Jack Tars, and you surely have met your fate. I hope you will meet with smiles and not frowns, as any girl should be proud of such a fine, handsome-looking chap as you, so sail in for her and my best wishes are for you."

I was very seasick for three days and did not leave my stateroom, but on the fourth day I got out, went to the saloon in the afternoon and sat at the table for the first time. It seemed like a family gathering, for the captain and his wife, the first officer, the ship's doctor and myself were the only ones present, as I was the only first-class passenger. There were a large number of steerage passengers.

The weather was very fine and we did not make much speed, owing to lack of wind, but I noticed that Mr. Charles E. Jack, the first officer, was all attention to me, and everything that he could do for my pleasure or comfort he did. When I went on deck he had always a nice place picked out for me, with some of his thick, heavy blankets to wrap about my feet if I needed them. He never went far away from where I was.

After we had been out about three weeks there was a very heavy gale, the ship rolled and plunged and the noise of the wind in the rigging was something terrible. I was nervous, too, being sick so long and frightened at the noises on deck and the powerful voices of the captain and mate shouting to the men. All was confusion and noise there. The storm lasted for twenty-four hours and we had to hold fast to the railing of the seats to keep from being dashed from one side to another.

The next night was beautiful and moonlight, but with a heavy sea, as the sailors called it. I went on deck to see the waves and as I stood looking over the stern watching the heaving of the ocean, I was startled by some one putting their arms around my waist and saying:

"Well, my little one, I have caught you alone at last. The stewardess tells me that you were very much frightened at the gale. I could not be with you, but you could not be hurt while I am near, for I would give my life to save yours if it had to be. I never saw a woman that I would care to call a wife till I saw you. We sailors are not accustomed to the fine ways of the dandies on shore, but what we say we mean, and all I have to give is a true, loving heart and a strong manly body to protect you. Nay, turn not away from me, for by the stars above I will have you, my fairy, my queen; my wife you must be, for I have dreamed of you years ago. Now, I have found you, my love, my all."

I said: "How long will we be on the water? When we get to shore you will go back in the ship and I will go to Manchester, to my people, and that will be the end."

"Nay, not so; I have signed a contract to take

the ship back to New York, then I will come and claim you."

I said: "When I tell you that I have loved another, you would not want me." He replied, "I do not care how many you have loved; you will love me for my kindness to you."

I told him all about Carl. He was very much hurt that a man would be such a brute as to strike a defenseless girl, whom he had called his love. He made no secret of his affection for me after that night. I did not know what to think about it. He was fifteen years older than I, and was the second son of Colonel Jack, who was a West Point cadet in his young days, but had practiced law for many years. He was a native of Philadelphia. His first wife, the mother of Charles, was born in Carlisle, Pa., so they were all Americans from away back. The family removed to Brooklyn, N. Y., in the early days and they were highly respected.

We were five weeks on the voyage and as we began to get near land my Yankee lover grew more impatient for me to say when I would be his. I admired him, for he was so frank and manly, but I had not the same love for him I had for Carl. I told him I wanted to think about it; that I liked him, but could not say that I loved him, and that if he took me he would have to win love from me, but I would be true and do the best I could to make life pleasant and happy.

When we got to Liverpool dear old Nursey was there to meet me. Mr. Jack was dressed up to see me safely on the train, so I introduced him to Nursey and she took a great liking to him. He saw us off on our way to Manchester. Then I told Nursey all about him, and she promised not to say a word to any of the family about it. The ship had been longer getting her cargo on board than was expected, so Mr. Jack came to see me on the Sunday before leaving and I was more than glad to see him, since Nursey had liked him so well, so I told him he would have to love Nursey, too. We went to Bellevue Gardens and strolled about until train time. Then he said: "I will be here for you about the 5th of September, and after we are married I will take you to my father's home till we see what we will do."

So he bade me farewell and was soon out of sight, the train starting as his feet were on the steps.

We were not long in Manchester, but went to the old home in Nottingham, where I had a very merry summer, only for Carl coming and writing his pleading, pitiful letters for me to forgive him and let him come and see me as of old.

I was still as confiding as I was years before, and would sit on Nursey's lap and put my head on her bosom and tell her all, reading Carl's letters to her. She would not chide me, but sympathized with me. She said:

"Just compare the truest one, a noble Godlike man, the other a sneaking coward, and there is no greater happiness on this earth than true love in a cottage, not fretting about notes or losses, but peace and confidence and happiness in each other. No, my child, I feel safe in giving you to this sailor, for truth is written in his face and he fairly worships thee."

I said: "Yes, and I promised him I would be true to him, and so I will. I am glad I told him all about Carl, for I would have felt guilty of deception if I had not told him all about it."

It was getting late, so we went to bed. I had not been long in bed when under my windows there was a beautiful sound of music and soft voices singing. They sang two or three songs, then suddenly all was changed, for Nursey had not retired and had caught sight of Carl and his companions, so she quietly went down the kitchen stairs and let "Nep," the big Newfoundland, loose. Some of them struck at him with their banjos, which made him savage, and he sprang upon them, knocking two of them down and going after the other; such yells and scrambling to get away was a sight to see. The next morning the lawn was strewn with pieces of coat-tails, neckties and pieces of hats, so between Nursey and "Nep," I got no more love-letters and no more serenades.

I had received letters from my Yankee sweetheart, in which he informed me that he had told his father all about his plans. The father was glad that his favorite son had confided in him, and was heart and soul with him in making arrangements for my reception. He wrote me to be sure and be ready, as that trip would be his last, expecting there would soon be war, as there was a great deal of dissatisfaction with the South.

On the 9th of September, 1860, the "Foster"

arrived at Liverpool. Nursey and I went to Liverpool on the 15th. Mr. Jack met us and took us to Birkenhead, where he had applied for a special marriage license. He did not get his until the 18th, and at 9 o'clock of the morning of the 19th we were made husband and wife, and he seemed to be the proudest and happiest man on earth. Nursey went back that night, as she had been away longer than she had expected.

My Yankee husband took passage for me on the steamer "City of Cork," as he had to take the "Foster" back to New York, so I bid farewell to my dear old England and all my kind friends and kinsmen and left for my new home and new life in America.

When I arrived in New York, Col. C. J. Jack met the ship to welcome me and took me in a carriage to his home in Brooklyn, where he had a young wife with two boys and a baby. She was about thirty years old and he was over seventy, which seemed strange to me. His house had a large brown stone front and was beautifully furnished.

They had arranged for a number of entertainments, so they set in with parties and receptions. I looked on and thought it was a strange lot of mixed people. The most of them wore diamonds and dressed in bad taste, and amongst them was a family who had made a large fortune in real estate. They had a house like a palace and wanted to outdo everyone. They gave a large party and had the most expensive things that money could buy. They had baskets of Piper Heidsieck champagne and had the finest cut glass decanters they could get. Madame put the champagne in the decanters, and when it was passed around, of course, it was flat and spoiled. I noticed many things were very much out of place, and I pitied the poor foolish people who exposed their own ignorance in such a manner.

My husband had now arrived home and C. H. Marshall, the owner of the Black Ball Line, had given him a ship to take charge of, so he was made a captain the first voyage after we were married.

Abraham Lincoln was elected President and there was great excitement and great confusion, and the Colonel was expecting to be sent as minister to Turkey.

The night before my captain was to sail there was beautiful moonlight. After supper we went out for a walk and when we got out of the thick settlement my captain said:

"My beautiful wife, I feel that I shall not make many voyages in my new ship, and that I shall be needed to help my country, for we surely will have war with the South."

I replied, "You surely would not leave and go to death without me being near you."

"If any traitor dares to try to tear down those glorious stars and stripes as long as I have a hand and arm left on my body I will strike back at him," was his answer.

We had stopped walking and stood under a tree, and as he said this he raised his hand to the sky, and as Nursey had said, he looked the

Godlike man, for he looked up to the stars and said this to himself:

"Yes, my next voyage will be to protect my country, so try, my darling, to give me courage to leave you, for that is all I fear. Since I have had you the world seems to have changed. I was a fast dare-devil before I met you, my loved one. Now I think of nothing but of how to make you happier, and when I come home and meet you with your smiles and open arms, God only knows what a heaven my home is. I think if anything was to happen to you and you were taken from me, I would not be long after you, for I could not bear to face the cold world with no one to welcome me or to care whether I came or went, excepting for what they could get out of me. My darling, you must help me, for the only sorrow that I could feel would be of leaving you."

We had continued our walk and by this time were at our door and said no more. The next morning he was gone with his new ship and I felt very sad and lonely, for something in his voice and manner seemed to leave me with a fear.

A few days after he had gone I received a letter from Nursey, in which she said my mother was getting ready to go to New Zealand, as her three boys had been sent there in Her Majesty's navy and there was a number of officers' wives and families going. My mother was sixty-two years old, but did not look over forty, and was extremely youthful in her manner. As I stood with the letter in my hand the tears rolled down my cheeks and I said:

"Farewell, dear mother, we shall never meet again on this earth, and I pray to all the powers in heaven to protect you and make you happy in your old age. You are on one side of this globe and your baby girl is on the other."

I felt very lonely and sad. Christmas was here and the children made merry, but many of the thoughtful people wore sad faces, as they knew not what the year '61 would bring. It was a very severe winter and many ships were lost. I was very uneasy, as my captain was behind the time due and I could get no tidings of him. I would lie tossing half of the night and calling on him just as though he could hear me.

One morning a telegram came saying his ship was off Sandy Hook and I felt as though a great weight had been lifted from me. He did not come until the next day, for the fog was so thick that the pilot would not take the ship to dock.

When he came he was sick and worn out with such a rough voyage. He had lost two men, whc had fallen from the rigging overboard. When he had been home about a week, on coming home one day he said: "I have resigned and turned my ship over to the owners. I am going to take an examination in a few days for a captain's certificate, so that I can take a captain's command in the navy, and hence I have put in my application. Our government has a very poor navy. They can get an army in a hurry, but not a navy, and they are getting ready on the quiet. They are enlisting all the men they can get, but as to the navy it takes time to make seamen, and land lubbers would be only in the way."

I made answer: "Well, my Yankee sweetheart, so you are going to leave me, and what will I do while you are gone? I do not like your father's wife, for she is very meddling and rude, and anything but a lady."

"She is not a lady," he replied; "she was our servant girl, but she got around my father and induced him to marry her. That is why my sisters do not come to the house."

He had three sisters, Harriet, Margaret and Lenora. Margaret was the most beautiful, queenly-looking woman I had ever seen, with a heart as cold as ice. Harriet was the wife of Major Snively, a beautiful character, and Lenora was single. She had gone with some friends on a trip to Paris, so I had not seen her.

"We will find a nice family out of town that I can board with," I said; "then I will be where it is cool for the summer."

The next day he took his examination and passed, receiving his commission in the navy later on. He had to get his uniform made to order, and all was life and excitement in getting everything ready, for he did not know where he was going or what vessel he would get. It was not long before the country was in arms, and it was wonderful where the soldiers came from in such a short time. The South had fired on Fort Sumter and war was declared.

Such excitement! It seemed as though everyone was crazy to go to war. Regiment after regiment was raised; the stores were as busy as they could be; the tailors weer offering larger wages and working night and day, and it was a common saying on the street: "We're spoiling for a fight and will wipe them off the face of the earth in six weeks." They little knew the temper and mettle of the South.

I was going to see a friend that lived out of town, a little way from the very trees where my captain swore that he would fight as long as he had an arm to fight with, and as I looked at the place I saw a man sitting under the same tree in tears.

I went up to him and said: "How do you do, friend?" He raised his head and looking up at me answered: "I have shed the most bitter tears this morning that I ever did in my life. Only to think that our flag has been insulted and torn down and my gray beard and head holds me back from joining the troops and resenting the insult."

"Fret not, for there are plenty of young men who will resent it," I answered. "All I have on earth is going. My husband put on his uniform on Sunday and is ready and awaiting orders."

The man replied: "Yes, and all I have I have given this morning," and he wept again. "I have two boys; one was old enough and he enlisted, but the other was only 18, and I went and signed for him to go in the navy, as that was his wish. Then I came out to this place to give vent to my sorrow, for I wanted to go, but they say I am too old. God knows I love my boys, but I love my country too, and they may come back all sound. Then I will have served God and country, too. But I will be the same as you, my lass; when my boys are gone I shall be alone, for their mother died four months ago. All my troubles have come at once."

"Cheer up and we will all pray that it will soon be settled,"I answered. His name, I found, was George Osborne.

I made but a short visit to my friend and returned home to find my captain waiting for me, and he said: "Well, I have got my papers to take charge of the 'Maria Carleton' in the bomb mortar flotilla of Admiral Farragut's fleet. Commodore Porter is in command, but we do not know where we are going, as we sail with sealed orders. Now, my darling, I shall soon have to leave you and it unmans me when I think of it. I was proud of my commission and went on board to give orders, but when I went into the cabin such a lonely feeling came over me. I took your portrait from my breast pocket and kissed it and then wept the bitterest tears I have ever wept in my life. Nay, my darling, the enemy's guns have no terror for me, but leaving one so young and fair, and in a foreign country alone and unprotected, breaks my heart and unmans me."

I threw my arms around his neck and said: "Come, my Yankee sweetheart, this will not do, for it seems to be a day of tears. I went to see a friend and saw a man weeping because he was too old to go to the war, and when I came to my friend's house I found them all in tears over the only son who had enlisted along with my friend's two brothers. Then I come home and find that my brave husband has been in tears. The South has surely sent her arrows straight home to us, for old and young seem to be grieved, but when you are gone from me I will talk to you as I do now and pray that you will come back to me safe and sound. But if you should fall I will try and get your body and lay it where I can come to you when life is ended, and I will call to your spirit to come and comfort me when I am lonely and in sorrow, and grief. So cheer up, for we will not be separated, either in life or death."

"Oh, my darling, if I fall and God will let my spirit come to you I will be with you, never fear," was his reply.

The next morning the First regiment left Brooklyn and it seemed as though everybody, old and young, had turned out to see them start. Every window was crowded and flags floated everywhere. The military bands were playing and thousands were in tears. The soldier boys with their new uniforms were a sight never to be forgotten.

The captain and I were standing on the street looking on when a soldier came up to him and grasping his hand said: "Well, my boy, we did not think that we would have to wear the uniform so soon." Then he turned and looking at me said: "My God, what does this mean?"

"This is my wife," replied the captain, "and it hurts me to have to leave her so soon." When I took a second look at the man I knew him to be the doctor on the "Foster," but he did not know that we were married. He was the doctor of the first regiment to leave. He fell into the ranks and was soon lost to sight in the crowd.

CHAPTER III.

IT was not many days later that the bomb flotilla was ordered into commission and all was rush and bustle. Provisions, guns and ammunition were put aboard and soon the men and officers were all ready and waiting for orders. It took ten days after the fleet was ordered into commission until it was ready, and everyone worked with a will. Half of the fleet had slipped out under sealed orders, for they did not want the enemy to know of their movements. My captain was going out when the tide was favorable, so the colonel and I went to the ship to say good-by.

As I stood on the deck I noticed a tall youth looking as pale as death and an old man with one arm around his neck and his hand clasping the youth's in farewell. When the old man turned to go I saw it was Mr. Osborne, so I went up to him and said:

"This is strange your boy should be one of my husband's crew." As I was talking to him the first lieutenant came up and I said to him: "I hope you will do me a favor. Do not let the sailors abuse this boy, and see that no harm comes to him."

"Ay, ay; I will be glad to do a favor for our captain's lady, and this lad is our cabin boy."

Both the boy and his father were spellbound with surprise and the captain came to see what

I was doing. The old man was choking with tears and could not speak, but went on shore and never once turned to look back.

I made merry as best I could, but the colonel when he said "Good-by, my boy," broke down and sobbed as though his heart would break, and it was some time before we could quiet him. Then my captain took me in his arms and kissed me. He was very pale, but said nothing for he could not trust himself to speak and I wanted to be brave so as not to worry him. All I could say was: "You will come back soon and I will be waiting for you, my Yankee husband. Be brave and true till we meet again."

We turned and were going down the plank when the boatswain came and piped us over as a mark of honor such as is given to distinguished people who visit a man-of-war. The carriage that brought us was waiting on the pier, and as my captain put me in first and helped his father, he choked back the tears that wanted to flow. As the carriage started he stood with his hat raised like a statue, and neither the colonel nor I said a word, for we were too full of grief.

I had kept up so as not to worry my captain, but as soon as I got all alone in my room I had a fit of weeping so that I thought my heart would break. All I did was to moan and sigh "He is gone; he is gone," and pray that God would bring him back safely.

A few weeks after the captain was gone I moved to Ravenswood, on the banks of the East River, and every morning as the troops went by I would wave my handkerchief at them and they would wave their caps and shout "Hurrah!" as though they were glad of a chance to give vent to their feelings after leaving their loved ones. I was patiently waiting for tidings of the fleet, for it had been gone some weeks when the papers said it was anchored near New Orleans, but no one knew why no attack was made on the forts. A few days after I got a letter saying that the spies had found out that the rebels had put chains with torpedoes on them across the river from fort to fort so that as soon as our vessels struck them they would be blown to pieces. That was the cause of the delay and our fleet did not know what to do.

Then my captain went to the flagship to see Admiral Porter, who had charge of the fleet, and said: "Give me a written order to go through the fleet and pick the men I want, and I will go under the forts and cut the chains, as it is the dark of the moon and there is no time to lose."

"This is a pretty risky business," said the commodore, "but all war is risky, and I will only be too glad to give you the order, but be sure and throw up your signal "All's well" if you are successful."

My captain got the men he wanted and took four long boats and all the tools necessary, and when he was about to start the cabin boy jumped into the captain's boat and said: "If you are going to your death, I will go, too, for I will not leave you."

So they started, and all his men were desperadoes from the Five Points of New York City, who would as soon kill as eat. They all swore by the captain to fight to the death and to kill the first man who showed cowardice. All night long they worked like lions, and the captain gave them whisky to keep them up. Just as the day broke—the last chain was dropped in the river and they had to row for dear life to get out of range of the guns from the fort.

They were seen by the rebels, who watched them through their glasses, and opened fire. My captain ordered the signal "All's well" run up and then our big guns began to bombard the forts. On getting back to his vessel my captain ordered the big mortar gun fired, and before the smoke had cleared away a ball from the fort struck the "Carleton" and passed through her powder magazine without exploding, but it threw my captain up in the air. He fell on his back on the deck and was stunned for a short time. When he came to, the cabin boy was wiping the blood from his mouth and the ship was in the thick of the fight.

It was certain the "Carleton" was sinking, so my captain gave orders to spike the guns and lower the boats. They got as much out of the ship as they could, and when the last boatload and the men had gone to the flagships my captain, the first lieutenant, the cabin boy and two sailors were forced to jump into the water and swim for dear life just as the ship began to sink. When they got out of danger they floated until the boats came and picked them up, taking them to the flagship.

When they got on board Commodore Porter

ordered my captain to take the place of the first lieutenant, who was killed, and the doctor and ten men were lying dead with him. Captain Jack was hurt internally and was drenched to the skin, but there was no time to change, as they were under a heavy fire all the time. The forts were firing as hard as they could and the fleet was getting nearer all the time, bombarding them with the fearful mortars and other big guns. Ben Butler was bombarding them from the shore and stealing all their silver spoons that he could get hold of, so you can imagine what a plight they were in. When the fleet finally got past the forts and into New Orleans my captain fell on the deck. He could not stand on his feet and the blood was pouring from his mouth. They had to wait until they could get a doctor, as many of the men were wounded and hurt and the doctors were very busy. The cabin boy stayed with him and did all he could to stanch the blood, bringing brandy from the officers' quarters. He bathed his forehead and was as gentle as though he were a girl.

When the doctor examined him he declared that his heart was hurt and that he never would be able to go under heavy fire again. He said my captain should not have stayed on deck as long as he did, and that it was a miracle he was not killed or had fallen dead from exhaustion.

The papers said that the "Carleton" had been lost with all on board, so I went to Brooklyn and found the poor old colonel nearly crazy with grief. I did not know at that time what had happened, and was as much shocked as the rest of them, but something seemed to say to me that I should see him again. I stayed at the Colonel's house that night, and such a night as I put in. The next morning I looked as though I had seen a ghost, but as soon as we got a paper we found it was full of the battle of New Orleans, and that it was not true that the "Carleton" was lost with all hands. The ship was at the bottom, but not the men, so we had our fit for nothing.

I did not like boarding, so I took a pretty cottage at New Rochelle and furnished it myself, so that when my captain came home he would have a home of his own. But months wore away and he did not come. I had a very good middle-aged Scotch woman living with me, and as I was expecting to become a mother I wanted my husband with me at such a time. Alas! that six weeks they were wiping out the South was the longest I ever saw.

I gave birth to a big baby girl and did not seem to recover from the effects for a long time after. I was just beginning to get around again and the weather was very cold when I got a telegram to come to Washington, as he was there. My captain had taken charge of the ironclad "Penobscot" and was ordered to the blockade of Galveston.

After a few months on the "Galveston," blockading, the Captain was ordered to Wilmington blockade, and was not very long there when he captured the iron clad steamer "Kate," trying to run the blockade, with a very valuable cargo on board. But that was not all; there was something on that steamer of a personal nature that belonged to General Robert E. Lee; it did not have anything to do with the North or the South, but was of the greatest importance to Lee, and let that be whatever it was, I never found out, but through that powerful order, Masonry, they buried the hatchet, the Blue and the Gray, and my Captain gave Lee whatever it was, then Lee took a diamond ring off his little finger and with tears in his eyes, said, "This comes next to my blood. If I fall strangers will get it, and only prize it for its value, but I feel sure your wife will have a higher value for it, seeing the date on the ring is 1314, over 590 years old, and has been in many strange adventures." Then he wrote on a bit of paper, "Please accept from a gentleman and an officer who wears the Gray. Robert E. Lee."

That very act showed the character of the man more than all his war record, for it showed a great, sensitive soul that had been touched by the kind act of a brother Mason; and more, it showed he was too much of a man to let such kindness go without showing his gratitude and appreciation and awarding something that was of a sacrifice for him to part with. I have carefully guarded the ring and will give it to the South later on.

I got ready and went, and when I got there the captain was present to meet me. The town was full of soldiers, the mud was a foot deep, and the little red ants in the hotel and all over the city were frightful. I went to the President's reception, was introduced to Mr. and Mrs. Lincoln, and shook hands with both. Then my captain came home and said he had a present for me. There were two dress patterns of black watered silk for Mrs. Lincoln and she took one and my captain took the other, paying $125 for it. I did not stay long, for my captain had to be away looking after the steamer, so we went back to New Rochelle. I had only been home a few days when a carriage came to my door and a tall man greeted me and said:

"Well, Mrs. Jack, I am a neighbor. I have just got my orders to go to Hart's Island as sutler, and I want you to take the tug boat which leaves every day at the foot of this street. Two tugs leave, one for Randall's Island, where the government has put all the sick and wounded, and the other to Hart's Island, where the recruits are drilled. I shall be the sutler there, and I was the shipping master that shipped your husband when he ran away and went to sea first. My name is Captain Ben Buck, and I would like for you to come to our opening, as the officers and their wives will have a dance and a good time. The military band will be there, so do come next Tuesday."

So I took the nurse and baby and a grip with my evening dress in and off we went. It was a beautiful day and when our tug got into the middle of the river there was the U. S. steamer with the recruits and bands and over 300 people on board. Mr. Buck was at the pier to meet me, as he had made arrangements for me to stay over night, and our tug got in first. As the U. S. steamer arrived at the pier the band struck up "The Girl I Left Behind Me," and a great cheer went up. All the island was down to see the newcomers and the recruiting sergeants with the fine figures, gay uniforms and assumed gayety made a fine appearance. They had come with the rest to have a good time.

I was taken to the officers' quarters and introduced and was surprised to find such a lot of frivolous women. They thought of nothing but their finery and who would be admired the most. Never a thought of the poor boys who were leaving their loved ones and might never see them again. After I had placed Nursey and the baby in good quarters I went around to see what I could do, and it made my heart ache to see the flower of our country's youth going to be shot down. Some of them I thought might come back with only part of their bodies, the other part shot away. Some looked so sad, others determined and some had a forced gayety.

When the news came of Andersonville prison, how they were torturing our boys with thumbscrews, turning their wounds that were full of maggots to the blazing sun, and how they were dying of thirst and pain, my soul bled for our brave and noble men. I wondered how many of the boys I had talked with that day were in the grasp of the demon Captain Waser—a demon in the form of a man.

Night came and I went to the ball, which was quite a gay affair. Young officers in their new uniforms were as gay as they ever were in their lives, and I got more than my share of attention. Several officers were very attentive, but my thoughts were on the poor boys who were outside, some of them looking on while others seemed to shun the gayety and wish to get as far from the music as possible. I was very glad when I got a chance to go to bed and get away from such a lot of unfeeling and shallow-minded people.

I passed the time the next day looking around, and when the boat came in I was glad to be on my way home. It was evening when the boat got to the pier, and as we landed I put the baby and nurse in the carriage so that I could walk. I sat for a time on the beach watching the tide rolling in, when I was startled by the moaning and crying of a woman.

I sprang to my feet and went to where the sound came from and found behind a large rock a poor woman, her eyes red with weeping. I sat down beside her and asid: "Let me help you, sister. What is your trouble.?

"I came on the boat from Randall's Island," she replied, "where my husband has had his leg taken off today, and when I left New York this morning I locked my three little children in the room, telling them to be good, for I was going to see their poor papa perhaps for the last time. When I was on the boat I found I had lost my last dollar, and as the fare to New York is 50 cents I cannot go tonight, but I will start and walk soon."

"I will give you a dollar," I said, "and if you come quickly we can get a train for New York."

So we started and had not gone far when a colored man came along with a cart, so I stopped him and got him to drive us as fast as he could to the depot, where we arrived just in time. I put that poor woman on the train and she left with tears and prayers for the beautiful kind lady who had sent her to her three little children, and I wandered back to my beautiful little cottage. I offered up a prayer for the poor distressed family and thanks that I had been the one chosen to give comfort to such great affliction, small as it was. Kind words and sympathy often lighten the burden of a breaking heart, so let us not pass any of them by, for we know not how soon some of our own may be afflicted. It was brought home to me by that poor woman.

I arose early the next morning and filled a large basket full of all kinds of vegetables and fruit and went to Randall's Island. I found the man Middleton, as that was the name of the woman's husband, and told him that his wife had gotten home all right, then I opened my basket to see what he would like, and he took a head of lettuce and ate it ravenously. So I gave him two more and asked him if there was anything more he wanted, but he said no. I then went to the rest of the wounded in the ward and it did me good to see the poor fellows eating the stuff I had brought them. It did not take me long to find out that they were crazy for green stuff, and after that I would go two or three times a week and take them what I thought they would like until the weather began to get cold.

In February the town became infested with burglars, who even went so far as to rob the church one night. One evening after putting Nettie to bed I was at the top of the stairs going down when I suddenly turned back and got my revolver. I do not know why I did this, but had a presentiment that all was not as it should be. I went downstairs and into the dining room. The door entering to the kitchen had a thumb latch on the kitchen side and a bolt on the dining room side and I had a big cat that would climb up and open the thumb latch with its paws when the door was not bolted on the inside. I sat down in the dining room and was reading a book very much interested when suddenly the latch was lifted. It startled me for an instant, but I thought it was the cat until I saw Tommy with his ears up like a dog and all attention. I turned my lamp down and got my gun ready, for the same feeling was within me that I felt at the head of the stairs.

I soon heard the latch again and knew that some one was trying to gain admittance. I thought of the gang of robbers the first thing and was very much scared. Then the feeling changed to one of determination, so I got up and went into the china closet, leaving the door ajar that I might see all that transpired. I had not long to wait, for they soon got the door open and two men with crape on their faces came into the room. One went towards the sideboard full of silver and glassware, while the other made for the parlor. Both had their backs to me and I pushed the door farther open and, taking deliberate aim, fired at the man near the sideboard. He turned and ran for the door and I fired another shot which sent the other man flying after the first. They ran up the street with me after them firing my revolver until help came and they were captured. A shot had struck one of the men, breaking his shoulder. They were locked up and I went home accompanied by two of the neighbors, who were afraid to let me go home alone.

The next morning it was discovered that one of the men was a prominent and well respected resident of the town, with a wife and family, and when the officers went to search the house they told the wife she would have to go to jail if she did not tell where the things her husband had stolen were. She became frightened at the thought of leaving her children all alone and told the officers the things were under the floor upstairs, but that they would have to move the bureau. When they did this they found jewelry, gold and silver and other valuables, which the officers took to a large dry goods store and left them to be identified by their owners. The prisoners were tried and the man I had shot, the well respected resident, got seven years in Sing Sing, but the other got only eighteen months, as this was the only robbery they could connect him with.

That spring the people of New York were greatly alarmed over the danger of cholera, and all who could get away left the city and moved to the suburban places, so that they could go in and attend to their business. They were looking for nice places such as New Rochelle, and there was no difficulty in renting a nice country place.

In the meantime my sister had written me saying one of my aunts had died, leaving us some money and property, and asking me to go back to England and look after it. So I put a notice in the paper that the house and grounds and furniture were to rent for $200 a month, and had not long to wait. A customer, a shipping merchant, rented the house for one year to take possession the first of May following. I got busy packing and my little girl helped me in her way, wanting to pack her little chickens and two little kittens, so that I had to watch her, and left the lids open until the family moved in and we were ready to start. The family moved in on the third of May and I took passage on the "City of Baltimore" of the Inman line bound for Liverpool. We had a very fine voyage and a very gay set of passengers. They had a banjo, violin and guitar, and would go on deck and play and dance in the moonlight until bedtime.

Among the passengers was an old gentleman who was very sick and had two daughters. I asked him if I could do anything for him and he said he had never been sick before, but could not get over the sea sickness. His name was Loveret and he was a wealthy merchant from Paterson, N. J., who was taking his two daughters for a trip to Europe after they had graduated. Two nights after I had seen him on deck his daughter came running into my stateroom saying her father was very much worse. I got up and dressed hurriedly, followed her to her father's stateroom, where I found he was dying. I went to the saloon and sent the steward in search of the doctor, then hurried back to the sick man. When the doctor came he saw that Mr. Loveret was dying and I passed the night with him, the end coming at 5 o'clock in the morning.

They were going to bury him at sea at sunset that evening, according to the custom, but I went to the captain and asked him to wait till we got to Liverpool, which would be only twc days. The captain went to the steward and told him to get a box ready to put the body in lock the stateroom door and give the keys to me. I went to the room every night and morning to see that all was right, as the two daughters were as helpless as children. When we landed I sent a telegram to his brother in Manchester, who came and took charge of the remains.

The customs house officers came for my keys to search my trunks and I was standing with a number of others looking on when they opened my large trunk, and the stench that arose from it was awful. When they began to remove the things they found three dead kittens that my little Nettie had packed up unknown to me with the idea of taking them to aunty. The passengers had a great joke at my expense, besides which it was an April fool for the customs officers, who had expected to find a human corpse, but were cheated out of a sensation. When I got to Manchester my sister and Nursey caught Nettie and said that she was their little Nettie over and over and that she looked just like I did when I was her age. They almost smothered me with kisses and it seemed more like home than ever before. My four brothers had enlisted in the navy and had gone to New Zealand, followed by my mother, who wanted to be near her boys. When she got there the officers gave a ball and mother was dancing up the middle and down the sides like a young girl, and that was the last we had heard from them.

We soon settled my aunt's estate. I got $10,000 in gold and some very valuable oil paintings and silverware, which I could not conveniently bring with me, and so left with my sister Liddy. She was going to take a trip on the continent, so I thought I would go, too, as Nursey said she would keep house and play mother to Nettie.

So we started and went to Burton and from there to Boulogne, then to Paris, where we got a very handsome suite of rooms for 10 francs a day at the Hotel de Louvre, having our meals where we wished. The next morning a man in a swallow-tailed coat and white necktie called at my room, bowing and talking in French. I could not understand a word and motioned for him to go, but he would not, and I became angry and threw my slipper at him, which he picked up and hugged to his breast. He bowed himself out and I went to Liddy's room and told her, but she laughed heartily, and said it was the garcon or waiter wanting to know if I would have tea or coffee.

I went out and sat on the balustrade to watch the flower girls and listen to the Italian boys playing their music. I went to the Tuillieries every day and spent an hour or two there in the picture galleries and on Sunday went to Versailles, where there are 100 fountains of different designs throwing water in every form imaginable. The Emperor went there on the first Sunday of every month and twelve bands played in his honor. The statuary was very fine and so was the old Emporor's palace, with its vast picture galleries and old relics of antique design, including breastplates, battle axes, spears and other weapons of war. We went with some of Liddy's friends to the Marbeal, a place where men and women were dancing like mad, the men on one side and the women on the other. They throw themselves into all manner of shapes and the dance is called the "can-can." We went to the Blondin circus one Sunday and were surprised to see priests there with black robes and square mortar-board caps, as they seemed to be out of place, especially on the Sabbath day. I counted five of them.

I was walking down the Champ de Elysees and had passed the arch of triumph when we met a funeral procession at which everyone stopped and the men took off their hats and bowed their heads and all the carriages and people halted until the procession passed. There were about twenty priests, four of them carrying the coffin and four ahead, the others following with heads uncovered, which showed that the French have a great respect for their dead. After dinner I took a stroll along the river bank and it seemed to me that all the old women had left their washing for Sunday and that seemed to be their washday. The beach was filled with women washing.

We left France and went to Switzerland, where we met a party of English ladies who were stopping at the same hotel. They said they were going over the Alps and wished us to accompany them, so we agreed to do so. They were twelve in number and we went on donkeys. Here I saw the most beautiful scenery that I ever beheld. When near the top we heard such strange sounds that seemed as though they came from the middle of the earth, but we were not long in finding out the real cause. When we descended on the other side we came to a large flat piece of ground covered with fig trees with their large leaves outspread and looking like umbrellas. Under one of these trees were three little boys playing different musical instruments, while about twenty other boys and girls formed a circle about them, dancing opposite to each other. It was a beautiful picture and no play in a theater could be half so nice. The girls wore short dresses and either blue or red stockings and very low cut shoes tied with the same colored ribbon as their stockings. They wore black aprons braided with the same color. Most of them were very beautiful, with fine olive complexions, soft blue eyes and round plump figures, with very small hands and feet. They were the peasants minding their sheep and goats. It was their dinner hour and they had met under the trees to eat their noonday meal. As soon as they saw us they ceased their dancing and began to sing their Swiss songs, which echoed over the Alps, and it was not long before a perfect swarm of sheep and goats came running down the mountain side in answer to the carol, which was a signal to them to come. We stood spell-bound watching the scene until they sounded another kind of note and the goats came and began butting our jacks, and one old lady with a big fan began screaming out for help. I was so full of laughter watching the old lady that I did not notice a big goat come behind my jack and give him such a bunt that I went sprawling over the jack's head.

The guide told us to give them some sous to call their goats off, so we gave them some and everything was all right. They had trained the goats in this manner in order to get money out of tourists, but they sang and danced for us for paying them and we went our way laughing at the tableau of the goats and the jacks.

We remained in Switzerland for two weeks, spending most of our time among the peasants and the sick. They used extracts of flowers for sickness, as there was not a doctor for miles around, and they seldom sent for one until the patient was beyond all earthly assistance. I saw them kill large fat dogs to extract the oil of them for consumption, and when the oil was treated it looked like hog's lard, and the patient soon got to like it and eat it on their bread instead of butter. I talked with a number of patients and they told me that it was a sure cure for consumption.

We went next to Naples and Mount Vesuvius, and every step we took we were annoyed with beggars. At the foot of the mountain were men to carry tourists up in chairs on two poles, four men to a chair. We arranged with them and they carried us up the mountain, stopping halfway at the Monks' Hut, where we had refreshments and found the reverend gentlemen very interesting. They had large St. Bernard dogs and would send them out to find men that had been lost in the snow of the mountains and they would bring him in dead or alive. Four of them would carry a man.

At times it is impossible to make the ascent on account of the lava flowing from the crater at the top, and the monks have to vacate in short order. We went out as near to the mouth of the crater as we could and it was dark when we returned.

We remained there four days, after which we went to Florence, where it was very warm and the people slept most of the day and would go on the housetops in the evening to get a breath of fresh air. The ladies wore lace dresses and black lace over their heads and the servants were all men. I would go out on the suspension bridge and watch the two classes of people going to and fro, the poor to their work and the rich to their homes. I went to the factories and watched the men and women plaiting straw for hats and bonnets and I visited the churches to hear the singing, which was very splendid. The weather was too warm to go about much, so we stayed there only five days.

Then we went to Rome and took in the sights of that great city. We visited St. Peter's cathedral, where there were 100 men and boys in white circular robes singing masses and vespers and the floor was marble and mosaic tiling of all colors imaginable. The walls were of marble covered with oil paintings of Scripture scenes, with magnificent statuary in all the nooks of the building. Down the aisle of the church there is a box a foot and a half long, one foot wide and one foot high, of solid gold, and said to contain the ashes of St. Peter. People of all nations come and bring their jewels and riches and lay them on this box and the Pope comes and blesses them. They are henceforth treasured as sacred relics. There is a lifelike statue of Christ as he was taken from the cross with the wounds in his side, hands and feet and the pallor of death on his face. One would almost think they could see the lips quiver to look at it and imagine that the look of death was real. There is also a statue of the Virgin Mary that is covered with jewels and precious stones which wealthy people have brought and strewn about, some having put gold chains about her neck with their names engraved thereon.

We stayed six weeks in Rome and then went to Cairo where the hanging gardens of Babylon once were. We took camels and Arabian guides and started across the sandy desert, the guides wearing loose white bloomers with full white gowns girded about the middle with red cord with two red tassels, red turkey hats and light boots laced nearly to the knee. They filled large skin bags with water and hung them on either side of the camels. We also took sacks and baskets of provisions and a skin of wine. We started and of all the journeys I ever made this was the worst, with hot sun and sandy desert. I was glad when we came to a hut where three monks lived and a little spring of water bubbled out of the sand. We stayed there all night and I was glad to have some kind of a change. We started back the next morning thoroughly disgusted with the monotony of the place and I made up my mind that the next time I started out to hunt scenery it would not be on a sandy desert. We left at once on our return to Paris, where we remained three weeks and then went back to Manchester, England.

While in Paris we went to the races about twelve miles out and the emporer and Empress Eugenie were present. We saw the famous race horse Gladiateur run and win the grand prize and a cup and the Empress Eugenie with her maids of honor made a grand sight on the stand. She was a handsome blonde and was dressed in amber colored silk with camel hair cloak, amber color, and her maids of honor were dressed in blue silk suits all one color.

When I got to Manchester I went to Chester to the races there. Chester is one of the oldest towns in England, with high walls all around and one can go up the steps and all around the city on the walls. On these walls they have museums and all kinds of shops for selling things and they are certainly 100 years behind the times in everything. We went to the races and there I found out the secret of how the betting men made their money on the races. They would start about eight horses, one of which was always a favorite; then they would take the field, laying odds against them all except perhaps the favorite, when the person betting had to lay odds on it winning. They would only have to pay one winner and win all the bets that were laid on the other seven.

We next took a trip to Wrexham, North Wales, on the River Dee. The Welsh are a very excitable class of people. The women wear wide-brimmed black beaver hats, shaped like a cove sugar loaf, broad at bottom and tapering narrow at the top, long cloaks with a yoke on the shoulders and full skirt to the bottom of their dresses. There were small thatched roof cottages plastered on the outside and kept whitewashed on the inside and outside, with a fine garden of flowers in front, with fruit and vegetables at back.

From there I went to Liverpool, where I met Nursey and Nettie. I then took steamer for Dublin and stopped at the Shelbies Hotel in St. Stephen's Green, taking my little girl Nettie with me. When I went out next day I was surprised to see such wide streets and a fine post-office on Sackfeald street, with five large stone pillars in front, and in the middle of the street and opposite the postoffice a large statue of Saint Patrick. The sidewalk was full of fashionably dressed people. I would rise early in the morning and take a walk in Peel's Park. On my way was a large Catholic church, with massive stone pillars in front, with large stone steps and a large arch forming a vestibule, the doors being quite a distance from the outer arch. This vestibule was full of women half clad and chilled from waiting for the doors to open so they could go in and attend their morning worship. The Irish seem to be more faithful to their religion than other people. It was Sunday and I had made some few acquaintances, among them three young ladies who were very rich; so we concluded to give the old folks the slip and go the rounds ourselves. We took a jaunting car and went to the Beggar's Bush Barracks, where the military band plays every Sunday in the park. We stayed there an hour, hearing the band and watching the parade. We then went to the lighthouse at Queenstown. An old woman called Peggy lives there; she was a jolly old lady and sat smoking a long clay pipe with sealing wax on the end. One of the girls gave her a shilling, when she brought out a little brown jug and a pot of milk and made some milk punch; when she poured the stuff out it looked like olive oil. I asked her what it was and she said it was pugeen; that she had made it herself out of barley and cheated the English government out of the duty. When I tasted it, it was very mild and tasted oily, but when I drank what was in the mug I thought I was on fire. The girls made fun of me. Peggy got another long clay pipe, which she threw on the floor and made a cross of the pieces. She danced the Fisher's hornpipe between the pieces and never touched them, being as nimble as a kitten, the girls keeping time with their hands and feet. When she got through she sang Irish songs. We stayed there for tea and had pickeletts and poached eggs, ham and pickled salmon, and tea as black as coal. We left there about eight o'clock, taking another mug each of pugeen, gave her a shilling apiece, got into the jaunting car and made for the city, singing all the way, the pugeen making us all feel jolly. It was 12 o'clock when we arrived at the hotel. The next day we went to Darrs Bally Mahone and the lakes of sweet Killarney, of which all kinds of ghost stories are told. It is a very fine walk and the hills around seem very romantic. If you shout out "Pat" the echo will come back "Faith."

Women were selling homemade Limerick lace and jewelry made from bog root, something like jet, but more of a dead black, carved in all manners and shapes. I visited many fine cottages; all had gardens. They burned turf instead of coal and I did not see the misery among them that I expected from what I had heard. They all seemed contented and happy. They asked me if there were any landlords in America. I told them "Yes"; that they had to pay rent for a small room at the top of a four-story house and if they did not pay rent every month they were put out. They said they thought they could get farms and houses free, but if they had to pay rent they did not think so much of our freedom.

We left and went to Cork, where I bade good-by to Nursey and sister and took the steamer "City of Cork" for New York.

We had a very pleasant set of passenegrs. One day I was playing a game of shuffleboard with the captain of the steamer, when the steward came and said they wanted him to come below and decide a bet. We went. It was a bet between two gentlemen that no one on board could tell what the seven wonders of the world were. The captain took off his hat and scratched his head and said he did not know, unless it was woman. They all laughed and then I was asked if I knew. I told them "Yes, that I had them in my pocket." That was too much for them; they roared with laughter; such a noise I ever heard. When I visited the museum on the walls of the "City of Chester," I opened a very ancient book called Santacupes, in which I found it stated what the seven wonders of the world were, and took a copy of them in a little memorandum book I had, and so I took my book out of my pocket and showed them what the seven wonders were:

First—Pyramids of Egypt.
Second—The Pharos of Alexandria.
Third—The walls and hanging gardens of Babylon.
Fourth—Temple of Diana at Ephesus.
Fifth—The statue of the Olympian Jupiter.
Sixth—The Mausoleum of Artemisia.
Seventh—The Colossus at Rhodes.

This decided the bet, which was won by the younger man. I was getting very tired of travel and longed to get home. I had written to Col. C. J. Jack, my father-in-law that I would sail on the "City of Cork" from Cork.

CHAPTER IV.

WE got to New York on a Sunday and as we lay in the river a rowboat came alongside; the gangway was lowered when who should come on board but my husband and Colonel Jack, with two brother officers and four sailers from his own ship, which was an agreeable surprise for me, as I thought he was far away. He had been transferred to the ironclad "Penobscot," when the war was over. They were all in their full uniform.

Captain Tippet of the steamer insisted on them all staying to dinner and went to the custom house with us.

Nettie did not know her papa. She called him the man with the big whiskers. We soon got through with the customs-house officers and went to Colonel Jack's house. We were there two weeks and then made arrangements to go to my own home, and mighty glad was I to get there again. The captain suffered very much from his hurt, and kept growing worse, so we went to live in Brooklyn, in order that he could get good medical attendance. A year after I had come home my second child was born, a fine bright boy.

The captain by this time had got worse, enlargement of the heart had set in and he could not lift twenty pounds. He had to get the greatest care, and everything was done for him that we could do.

I went to speculating in real estate and was very successful. I started in with $5,000 and in fourteen months I made $30,000.

I thought the captain would get better if we went to Chicago and we concluded to go and buy a farm. So I sold the house we lived in and kept our piano and the best of our furniture and had them packed for shipment.

My baby now took sick and as the people who had bought the house were now moving in the captain took rooms in a hotel. Nettie, who was now five years old, was taken down sick with scarlet fever. We moved out on a Tuesday and my boy died on Friday and was buried on Saturday.

When I came back from the funeral I sat down on Nettie's bed and was crying, when Nettie told me not to cry, as she was going to her brother. I said:

"You will not leave mamma all alone, will you?"

She said that when they took her brother away she tried to say her prayers, but could not, for the angels came and told her they would take her to her brother and showed her such pretty flowers.

"Don't cry, Mamma, but pray; and when I have got on my new white dress and in the nice coffin like brother, see that the curls on my forehead are fixed nice, as I want to look nice when I join the angels."

She closed her eyes and the captain came in in about an hour with the doctor. She asked him to kiss her and to lay her head on my bosom.

I took her on my knees, thinking that she had gone to sleep and was going to put her in bed, when I saw she had gone to sleep forever.

I laid her down, and pen cannot describe the bitterness of my soul. I did not cry now, neither could I pray. I thought God had not been just to me, as there were so many children with cruel parents, whom death would have been a blessing to, and yet they were spared to their misery, while my children, whom I loved, were taken from me. We buried our Nettie on Sunday from Theodore Cuyler's church, in Greenwood cemetery, Brooklyn. The saddest thing of all was to have to leave them, as we were all ready to start for Chicago.

When we arrived in Chicago and looked at the farm I found it was not what it had been represented to be and would not buy it; so returned to the city and went into the wholesale grocery business, but did not do very well, the captain not knowing much about business. He had been to sea all his life and did not know anything about buying goods. We soon lost quite a sum of money.

We were there two years when my third child was born, a girl, and when she was three months old, the captain bought a large stock of goods, part of which was delivered when our stable caught fire, which set fire to our house, we having a narrow escape, myself, baby and the servant girl being taken out of the fire by the men. Some of the furniture and the horses and the carriages were saved. Our loss was about $20,000. I afterwards traded the horses and carriage for two building lots, and some time after, when I tried to sell the lots, on getting an abstract, found that the party I had bought from had sold them the day before to another party, and when I went to look for him I found that he had left the country. His name was Frank Buckley. I had only two lots, which I had bought cheap away out near the stock yards. We left Chicago thoroughly disgusted and went to Brookville, Kansas, where we bought a tract of 320 acres of land from the National Land Company. We built a large double house, planted fruit trees and bought some cows, hogs, horses and farming utensils. One day on going out to the well, where Jenny, my little girl, was playing, I saw a large snake, an adder. I took a pitchfork and ran it through the head and threw it to the hogs, as I knew they would kill the rattlesnake. To my surprise the hogs all crouched in a corner and were afraid of the snake. I called the hired man, who told me it had a very poisonous sting in its tail, which the hogs knew, and that was why they were afraid.

I took very sick with chills and fever and could not live there, so we traded the farm and everything for a house and two acres of ground in the suburbs of Brooklyn, and went there.

After we got to Brooklyn the captain wrote to Admiral Porter to help him get a position, as Admiral Porter always stood by his men. After the war Congress passed a law that service men should have preference for government positions, so Admiral Porter wrote to Rear-Admiral Smith to give Captain Jack a position in the Brooklyn

Capt. Jack at One of Her Mines.

navy yard and make a vacancy for him at once. So the captain of the watch was dismissed and Captain Jack put in his place.

In the meantime I had gone to housekeeping and made a trade for a house and lot away out on the line of Brooklyn and East New York. As the captain got his pay every month I kept buying lots and speculating. I built a house with bay windows and all modern conveniences and had a beautiful homelike place. I began to think again that life was worth living.

One day the captain came home and was very sad. I wondered what could be the cause, so I asked him and he told me he was ordered to do a thing which he did not like to do and it troubled him very much.

At that time there was great excitement about the Spaniards sinking one of our vessels, along with a large number on board. Our government had demanded an explanation from the Spaniards, and in the meantime two large Spanish man-of-war ships came into the Brooklyn navy yards for repair. One of them had got out and they wanted to hold the other one until there was a settlement for the United States ship (the "Merrimac") that had been sunk.

If we went to war over the affair the "Ariapolis" would do great damage to our navy, as she was a fine vessel, well manned and equipped. In retaliation for the loss of our vessel, they wanted the "Ariapolis" blown up, as she was ready to sail, and word came to the navy yard not to let her go out until further orders. She was at one of the docks and ready to start.

They got powder and everything ready to blow her up. This was on Saturday. The captain said it was a disgraceful act and little less than murder, and that it would bring disgrace on the United States, and that he would either have to blow up the vessel or quit the service. I said nothing. I dressed up in boy's clothes and went to the navy yards and on board the "Ariapolis." They had been at mass and were gambling in the officer's messroom. I thought it would be a dreadful shame to blow up so fine a body of men when they were not to blame. It looked like gaining a man's confidence, asking him to your house and then murdering him, and it would truly have been a disgrace to our nation, for as the "Ariapolis" came into our yards in peace it should be let go in peace, and if they made war they should give her a chance for her life.

I procured the password from the captain. He did not know I was going out. I was determined the vessel should not be blown up. The powder was placed under her, the fuse was laid and my captain was to touch it off. I took my pocket knife and cut the fuse in four or five different places, and took a piece of the fuse about a yard long and put it in my pocket, and left everything so they would not know it had been disturbed. I started home, but had to pass two watch guards and give the password, which was "Nelly Grant." I climbed over the walls and walked home, as the cars did not run after two o'clock.

When I got home I did not go to bed, but sat

thinking how I could prevent her getting away. The captain came in, in the morning and told me something was wrong, for the fuse had been touched, but did not explode the powder.

I hit on a plan to prevent her from going out. It was to sink one of our old boats at the mouth of the dock, so that the big man-of-war could not get out until the boat was raised; and they could take their time in raising her. After breakfast the captain went to the navy yards and gave his plans to a superior officer, who agreed with him at once. So a coal barge was took up to the dock and tied. The captain went on deck and took her pumps off and cut a block out of her bottom and left it, so that when night came he took the block out and went to the watchhouse. She sank two hours after.

So the "Ariapolis" was a prisoner without any disgrace to our nation or any innocent lives lost.

The next day I told the captain what I had done and showed him the piece of fuse I had taken as a relic. He was very glad I did it. After some parleying the Spaniards paid all damages; the coal barge was raised and the "Ariapolis" went away, its crew in ignorance of how near they were to eternity and that they owed their escape to the actions of a woman.

All was now sunshine in our little home, and in March a baby girl was born. Our gardener neighbors all sent a pot of flowers and it so happened that they were all daisies of different colors, so we named the baby Daisy, and well she deserved the name, as she was the most beautiful child I ever saw. All went well with us. I bought and sold real estate and made money very fast.

One week before Christmas the captain came home and said his father was very sick and had been calling for me all the time.

So I took Daisy and went to see the Colonel. When I got to him I thought he was asleep, and sat down by his bedside for about an hour, when he said:

"Why don't she come?"

I said, "Who do you want to see, pa?"

"My daughter Nelly," he said.

I told him I was here. He asked me to put my hand on his forehead, and he closed his hands as in prayer and said:

"God, have mercy on her, have mercy on her. When her poor, kind fair face is smiling her poor, sad heart will be breaking."

He prayed God to protect and comfort me in my hours of sorrow and affliction. He said:

"Nelly, if you could see what I see, my poor girl, you know not what is in store for you, and what sorrow is before you. Come in front of me, so that I can see you."

I did as he told me, but he went off to sleep again, while I sat beside him and thought over what he had told me, thinking he must have been dreaming, for I had not a trouble in the world; everything was bright and cheerful with me; this world never seemed so beautiful to me before.

At nine o'clock in the evening he opened his eyes and looked for me. He said:

"I am going; good-by, and may God comfort you in your hour of need." Those were his last words. He had breathed his last.

Captain Jack took his father's death very much to heart, and his old heart trouble grew worse. He got so bad he could not lie down, as he would choke if he did. He had the best medical aid I could procure. The doctors held a consultation and said his heart had gotten so enlarged that he could not live; that dropsy of the heart had set in. He suffered dreadfully until the end came. I had not gone to bed a night since his father's death. I had many weary nights with him. Sometimes the Free Masons from his own lodge would sit up with him, but I would not dare undress and go to bed. When he would fall asleep in his big, easy chair, I would lie down on the floor and take a nap. Toward the last of his illness my little Daisy would say:

"Dod bless poor dear daden."

She could not speak plainly yet.

On the fifteenth of June the captain was raving and I had a fearful time with him. After a time he became quiet and I lay on a lounge in the room. I thought I saw his father and my little Nettie standing beside him and waiting for him to get ready for the journey. Our little boy came and threw flowers at his feet, and the American flag was all ready to throw over him.

I jumped up with a start and when I did the captain said:

"I wish you would send for all of my men that

can come to see me, for I am going to die, for I saw our Nettie, and she said:

"'Come, papa, come and leave this world of sin and sorrow and come to your God.'"

So I sent a messenger to the navy yards to tell all the men to come that could. He told them he was going to die and leave them, but that heaven would not be heaven to him until his wife came to him; and that he knew Daisy would soon follow him. He spoke to his men very calmly; most of them were in tears. Then the rector of the Trinity church came and administered the sacrament to him for the last time on earth. We were Episcopalians, and all our children were baptized in that church.

At six o'clock he went on his long journey, never to return in flesh and blood.

I laid him out on the floor and watched over him, for I wanted to do these last sad rites myself. I could not bear to have another touch him. I sent to the city for the undertaker, and Daisy and Captain Black Cat were all alone with him that night; Daisy had fallen asleep.

At six o'clock the undertaker came. When the casket was being carried down stairs the old black cat set up a terrible squall, and kept it up for some time. The corpse was put in the parlor and the cat came and lay under the casket; it would not eat a mouthful until after the funeral. She followed the corpse to the grave and I never saw her after.

The Free Masons conducted the funeral; they were in full uniform and acted as his pallbearers. It was the most solemn scene of my life. The choir sang, "Jesus, lover of my soul," and "I would not stay away from Thee."

The minister spoke about how he came by his death, his bravery in the war, what he had suffered from his injuries and what a kind husband and father he had been. He said he hoped the men would live as Captain Jack had done.

We took him to Evergreen cemetery and laid him in the receiving vault, until I had decided on a plot of ground.

When all was over I felt as though I had lost one of my arms, I was so crippled. I did not know what to do. I would go from room to room and not know what I wanted. Even the animals and the chickens seemed to know there was something wrong. Even my garden seemed to fade and the flowers to droop. I could not take an interest in anything. No pen can describe the feelings of loneliness and desertion that came over me at the table. To see the vacant chair at the head, no more rejoicing over papa's bringing home nice things from town. I prayed that if my husband had ever done a wrong in his life, for God to punish me for it and spare him. I would take my children every Sunday morning to the cemetery and sit and watch the vault where he lay, until the fall came, when I began to arouse myself as if from a dream. I had my two little girls to educate and provide for, and found I still had a mission in the world.

I began to look around me to lay some plans for the future.

CHAPTER V.

I WENT through Prospect Park and on the boulevard on the junction of Coney Island road, where there was a very fine tract of land. I made inquiry as to the owner and price, and was informed it was $60,000. I soon made a trade for the land and paid a portion of the money down. I then proceeded to build a large hotel on it, with marble tiling, and fitted it up very handsomely. It cost me $40,000, with stables and outbuildings, and when I opened it I had a tremendous run, which gained me the envy of the other road houses, for several of them had to close, as I took all their custom. I bought my own material and had it built by day work; that is, I did not let it by contract, and it was a source of great annoyance to me. I bought $2,500 worth of silverware and had gotten into the house when I had to go to town. Coming back, driving through the park, I saw a big fire and thought it was the car stables. I met a park policeman and asked him where the fire was, when he told me it was the Bon Ton. That was the name of my hotel.

I whipped my horses, and they, being spirited animals, went full speed. When I got there I asked for my children and was told they were in the burning building and that the firemen could not find the room they were in. There

Capt. Jack's Fort in the Woods.

was a second-story balcony. I asked a tall man to help me to get up on the balcony. He gave me a hoist. I got on his shoulder and made a jump, catching the railing, and pulled myself up and got into the hall. The smoke drove me back. I tore off a piece of my dress and tied it over my face, so that the fire would not burn my face, and crept on my hands and knees along the hall, counting the door jams as I would feel them with my hands, until I came to their room, which was locked. I braced my feet against the other side of the hall and with a desperate push with my shoulders I burst open the door. I then rushed to the window and found that I could not open it. I put my foot through it and broke the sash. Then I went back to the bed and got hold of the nurse girl. She would not move. I took her out of bed, dragged her through the window and threw her over the balcony. She was caught below. I went back and got my two children and took them out on the balcony, and by this time the people had got a cloth for me to drop them in. I dropped Jenny first and then Daisy, and they were caught without injury. Instead of dropping, I got on top of the railing and jumped. I got on top of the railing and jumped into the air. I had become excited as the people were hollering for me to jump; that the roof was going. I broke two ribs and my ankle. I did not jump too soon, for as I made the leap the roof went in with a crash, and they barely saved me from the flames. I was taken to a neighbor's house and it was a long time before I was able to be around.

I was unable to put in proof of loss to the insurance company in time, and when I did they would not pay me. I commenced suit, lost it, carried it to a higher court and was defeated there, when I carried it to the Supreme Court. I had lost all my money and business, and it cost me no little amount in carrying the case up.

I applied for a pension and had about given it up when it came. I had been notified that I had to take the captain out of the vault and it worried me very much. When my pension came I was paid back to the time of the captain's death. I went to the cemetery and bought a very nice plot and the next day I went with my two little girls and buried their papa. We were all alone except the men who buried the body. Daisy looked very sad and after they had finished and gone she gathered a lot of wild flowers and laid them on her papa's grave.

I took a suite of rooms that were not in the most fashionable part of the city. I was waiting to see what would be the outcome of my lawsuit with the insurance company, and waited three years. I found that my friends gave me a wide berth after I lost everything; a bitter experience not shared by me alone.

Then I began to see that the only friend on earth was money, and not only a friend, but power; that I must stir and do something, or go somewhere. I was in a brown study, thinking what was best for me to do. Christmas was near, and I was determined I would not wait longer; that I would do something in the spring.

Christmas came and the children hung up their stockings, and in the morning they were full of nice things. When I got up I found Daisy had filled a peach basket full of cake and other things and had gone out with them. The morning was bitter cold. I was angry with her and intended punishing her when she came back. On her returning, I asked her where she had been. She told me she had been to an old woman, who had no breakfast and no fire, and that Santa Claus did not take her anything, so she had taken her part of the things that Santa Claus had brought her. I did not know any such woman. When dinner time came, Daisy took all of her turkey and put it away for the old woman. I told her to eat her dinner and I would take some dinner to the old woman. I put up a large plate of dinner and Daisy led me about a block away to a basement, where, sure enough, I found an old woman without fire or food, just as Daisy had told me, with a straw bed on the floor, an old chair, and a little rough pine table. But the place was clean. I gave her the dinner I had brought and she told me she had laid down and never expected to get up again, and that she had not tasted food for over two days when my little Daisy was running after a little kitten and her door had blown open. She got up and saw Daisy with a large homemade biscuit. She went into the basement with the old woman, who told her she was hungry and cold and that Daisy had given her her biscuit and brought her a basket of nice things.

Daisy would take her something to eat every day, and one day she gave her ten cents that some one had given her; and all that had kept her alive for ten days past was what the child had brought her, whom she looked upon as an angel sent from God to save her life. She wept most bitterly and said she was weeping Christmas morning when a gentle rap came to the door and there stood the little fairy with her basket. I was poor, but could spare a little, so I sent her some coal and a dollar. I was singing in the choir of the Methodist Episcopal church and told some of the members, who went and gave her aid.

Nothing unusual transpired and now it is February and the weather is fine. On Sunday I felt as though I could not sing in the choir that day. It seemed as though a cloud was hovering, though I did not know why. The children went to Sunday school and it was late when they got home. Jenny told me the superintendent said:

"Who can doubt there is a God when we see such people as there are before us?"

And he said to Daisy:

"You are the little pink of the flock."

And she said:

"No, I ain't; I'se a daisy."

The children had gone to bed that night. I was sitting reading, when I thought I saw a black cloud go out of the room and pass into the bedroom. I started to my feet and went into the bedroom where the children were asleep, but I could see nothing. I sat down again and began reading. I had hardly got started when I saw the same thing again. I wondered what it all meant, when it came again for the third time. I lit the gas in the bedroom and went over to the bed where the children lay. I saw that Daisy was in a great fever. She awoke and asked me for a drink of water. I gave her a drink and she went to sleep. I went to bed with the children, but I had soon to get up again, for Daisy wanted water every few minutes, and when daylight came I sent for the doctor. When he came he said that the old enemy, scarlet fever, had come again. I brought her out and made her a bed on the lounge in the sitting room and at twelve o'clock noon she went into a spasm. I wrung my hands and screamed and was heard for blocks. The neighbors ran in to see what was the matter. I was as white as death and cried:

"Oh! why has God punished me so? What have I done to deserve this affliction, and he robbed me of my family? Ah! my Daisy! My Daisy!"

The doctor came, but could do nothing. She came out of her spasms and called "Mamma." I came and sat by her. She looked into the corner of the room and said "Papa." I said, "Do you see papa?" She smiled and said:

"I'se coming papa; I'se coming. I am going to papa. Don't cry mamma. Come, let Daisy kiss your poor white face." I kissed her and in less than three minutes she was dead. I thought I would go mad. My poor Daisy, who was the pink of the flock at Sabbath school the day before, was now cold in death. I was calm in all my troubles before, but now I felt like raving. After the captain's death I had prayed God to punish me for the captain's sins if he had any, and let his soul rest in peace; but I never dreamed of such punishment as this. I clasped my hands to my heart, for I thought it would jump out. I thought of what Colonel Jack had told me on his deathbed, "That when my poor, fair face was smiling, my poor, sad heart would be breaking." If any one could have experienced my grief they would have prayed to God to spare me and keep them from suffering the same. No pen can describe my misery. If I were crucified I could not have suffered more nor half as long. I sent for the undertaker and told him I had no money, as my three months' pension was not due until the 4th of March. He said never mind, he would attend to everything, and so I sat that night all alone with my Daisy I thought of her and of all the good church people and wondered if there were any among them who would take their Christmas gifts and Christmas dimes to a poor old starving woman and go without themselves, and now my Daisy was gone and I had not a cent to buy flowers for her coffin—the least gift that could be given—and she used to fill her apron with flowers and take them to poor dear papa's grave. The next day the undertaker came and brought her one of the handsomest caskets he could get and a box of the choicest flowers, which he laid upon her breast. It seemed as if he had read my thoughts. It was a very chilly day and we buried Daisy beside her papa. I could not bear any noise after she had gone; if a door was shut quickly it would startle me.

The same night, after laying her by her papa, I could not go to bed and shut my door and lock her out. It seemed as if she would come. While sitting with sad forebodings I composed the following lines:

> Close the door gently,
> Bridle thy breath,
> My little earth angel
> Is talking with Death.
> Gently he wooes her,
> She wishes to stay.
> His arms are around her,
> He leads her away.

Summer came, but it brought no sunshine to my home. Jenny would say:

"Mamma, why don't you sing? You look so sad and your face looks so pale since our Daisy died, and you never go to church any more."

I could no longer stand the sight of children, for every time I saw them the thought of my Daisy being taken would unnerve me. I fell away to almost a skeleton. I could not rouse myself. I would go to the cemetery three or four times a week after Jenny had gone to bed, when the evening was cool. I had made a nice garden in my burial plot and when the evenings were cool I would sit there and console myself with the thought that this one spot on earth was mine, and the spot where all I held dear was laid. I would often sit there until twelve o'clock at night and go home on the last car. I was so much taken up with my own sad thoughts that I did not notice people watching me. I always wore a white wrapper and a little black hat, which I would sometimes carry in my hand and use it for a fan. Toward the last I noticed several people looking toward the cemetery, but paid no attention to them. One bright moonlight night, quite late, I was coming out, and when I got to the gate two men stood still, until I opened it, when they started on a run. When I got to the corner there was quite a crowd of people there, and when I came near they got out of my way as fast as possible. I stood still, wondering what it could mean, when two men came halfway to meet me and said, "In the name of the Almighty what do you want?" I said:

"I want nothing but my own. My husband and my children lie there in the cemetery and they are mine."

One said:

"Are you flesh and blood, or are you of the spirit?"

I said:

"I am like yourself; I belong to this earth."

I thought that if I could not go and see my dead darlings' graves without being taken for a ghost, I had best stay at home, so did not go again for some time.

Summer went and winter came, but it brought no joy to my lonely home. I would sit for hours at a time half dazed, thinking, my senses far away.

One day in spring Jenny came in and said she had invited two little girls to tea, as Saturday was her day home from school. She had seen nice lettuce in the market and asked me to get some. It was snowing, so I took my umbrella and was on my way to the market when a child caught in a heavy door that had been blown shut by the wind. I dropped my umbrella and ran to catch the child, but was not quick enough and she was knocked senseless. I took the child in my arms and was carrying it upstairs, the house being a French flat, when a stout old lady came out of flat No. 7 and said the child belonged to flat No. 3. She rang the bell of that number, when the mother came running downstairs for the child and took it out of my arms. As a was turning to go away, the stout lady said to me:

"I would like to speak to you, if you will just step in for a minute or so."

I went in and saw four old ladies sitting around a table; one of whom jumped up and said:

"Thanks to the good spirits; she has come at last."

I thought I was caught in some trap and that the place was a private mad-house. I said:

"You have the advantage of me; I don't know any of you."

One of them said:

"But we have known you for years, but never saw you before with our natural eyes. We saw you with our spiritual eyes and want to ask you some questions before you leave us." I said:

"I hope you will not keep me long, as I have left my house and three little girls all alone in it."

They asked me if I was much of my time with the sick, and if I had ever noticed I had much power over them. I told them it seemed to come natural for me to know how to take care of them, and if any of my church people were sick and poor I always went and helped them, and was very fortunate in relieving their ills. The stout lady came over to me and said:

"I have a daughter nineteen years old, and the doctors have given her up. She prays she will pass away with her senses; she has such pains in her head and thinks that bees are stinging her. We are spiritualists and the spirits tell us you can help her. You must try, as we will not let you go until you see her." I asked where she was, and was told they would send for a carriage and take me to her. I did not want to go, on account of leaving my house and the little girls alone. They then sent for a carriage to take one of the women to my house, to stay with the girls until I came back. They got another carriage and took me out to Henry street, to a large brown stone front house.

We went upstairs, and there sat a most beautiful girl, crying out, "O! my head! my head!"

I went to her and said:

"I will help you soon." I told the carriage driver who was in waiting to go to the brewery and get a sack of malt that was left after brewing, and when he brought it I put it in a wash boiler and put it on the range, with water enough to make it like thin mush, just hot enough to bear my hand in it. I then took it to her room, stripped her, put her feet in it and rubbed it all over her. She had Bright's disease of the kidneys, and was full of water, and dropsy of the heart had set in; the water on the brain caused the pain and the light-headedness. I saw all this as soon as I saw her. As I worked with her the water began to ooze out through the pores of her skin like out of small faucets. I did not dry her, but rolled her in a blanket and gave her some brandy and milk. In fifteen minutes she was fast asleep and the water was all out of her system.

I knew it was only temporary relief and that she could not live, and would fill again. I went home, and in five days they sent for me with a carriage to come at once. I went, and I never saw such a beautiful scene; one that I shall never forget. She lay in bed, and the bed was covered with flowers of great beauty. It was in April, and flowers were very expensive, but the most costly were there. Women and young girls were kneeling around the bed, singing in a low tone—"The Sweet Bye and Bye," and Oh! so sweet and plaintive!

When I entered, the poor, dying girl held out her hand to me and said:

"My prayers have been granted; I have my senses. Thanks to you for your help. I hope to meet you on that beautiful shore; join us."

I knelt down and helped in the chant. She

tried to sing, but could only say "The sweet bye and bye," and her spirit had gone to that beautiful shore. I stood looking on and thinking how solemn, grand and beautiful was that dying bed. No tears nor mourning, but passing away amidst hymns, flowers and song.

I found out that my new-made friend, the mother of the girl who had just passed away, was the great Madam Clifford, the greatest spiritual medium of the day. She clung to me as if I belonged to her. One day I was there and she went into a trance and I was very much surprised when she described Captain Jack and the clothes he was buried in, as I knew she had never seen him and knew nothing about him. But when she told me that I was a Rosicrucianist, and was born to find hidden treasures, my thoughts went back to my childhood days, when the gypsy queen had said the same thing. This was really something I could not understand. I had many hours' talk with her after that, and tried to investigate how she gained her knowledge. But the more I thought about it, the deeper the mystery became to me, and I asked myself if it were best for us to know our future; or if it would add anything to our happiness to try to find out the mysteries of the other world, and leave the matter for those to solve who took more interest in it than I could.

I was satisfied in my own mind that the spirit could come back to this world again at some time or other and that we have spirits around us all the time—either good or evil—and that they influence us; and in a matter of justice our first impressions are always right; also, in our daily business transactions, many times, when I speculated in real estate and bought on the first impressions, I always made more money. But if I would stop to consider and take advice, and waver from first impressions, I was sure to lose. So I soon learned to use my own brains for my own business and leave others to do the same.

I went and had a talk with my attorneys, who I must confess were quite an exception to the general run of attorneys, were good and honorable gentlemen—Riley & Wineberg, of Brooklyn—and told them I thought of going West, and putting my little girl in a good boarding school, so I set about getting ready to start, and in a week had everything ready. I went to my sister-in-law, the wife of Dr. Quackenbosh, and asked her to look after my Jenny. Then I went to Denver. When I got there early in the morning I went in search of a restaurant. The postoffice was on Fifteenth and Larimer streets, and after wandering about for more than an hour I got into a restaurant on Holiday street, and while I was getting my breakfast colored men began to come in and I saw that I was in a negro dive. I paid the 50 cents they charged, then went away to the outskirts of town on Champa street, where I found two nice rooms situated between Fifteenth and Sixteenth streets. The next door was a laundry with a 50-foot lot and they wanted me to buy it for $250. A few days afterward while walking down Sixteenth street some one shouted "Captain Jack!"

I turned to see whom it could be when a lady very handsomely dressed came toward me with extended hand. I did not recognize her as anyone I had ever met before, but she said, "You don't remember your nurse-girl, Jennie?"

I said, "Well, you do not look like the same girl, but I am glad you have married so well, for judging by your dress your husband must be a wealthy man."

She walked to my rooms with me and I told her of the captain's death and my losses, saying I thought of going to Leadville. She advised me not to go there, but to go to a new valley being opened by the government, an Indian reservation named Gunnison. She said there were so many chances to make money there that I decided to follow her advice, when my week was up at my room, as I had paid the rent in advance. Then Jennie left me, saying that she would return the next day to tell me something. I waited until she came and then she told me a sad story. She had married after leaving me. Her husband, after a few months, began to stay out at night and would beat her when he came home. One time she followed him to see where he spent his nights and discovered that he was frequenting a large sporting house. Jennie got in the back yard and saw her husband with his girl all love and smiles.

When he came home he greeted his wife with curses and blows and for many days practically drove her to starvation. Then she said, "So this is the reward of a true, virtuous wife. Men leave their wives for these painted, lying women."

Then she fell on her knees and prayed God to forgive her, and with uplifted hands swore she would enter a sporting house and wreck the life of every man she could to avenge the wrong that had been done her, and it was the big swell house of Madame Clara Dumont on Holiday street she entered.

"Now," she said, "men come to my house all smiles with their money and when their cash is gone they are politely shown to the door."

She asked me to come and see her before I left. It was nearing dusk when I entered a fine appearing house on Holiday street. The lights were burning brightly, and when I rang the bell a man in white jacket and apron opened the door. He seemed surprised when I told him I wanted to see the madame, for I had forgotten the name she told me. When he asked my name I was in a predicament, for I did not want anyone to know that I had entered the place. So I replied, "Tell the madame I am the lady from New York who is going West."

He left me standing in the hall and went upstairs. In a moment Jennie came running down to me and took me to her rooms. She had nine ladies, as she called them, summoned to the room and to them she imparted the secret of who I was. She told them that I was her mistress before she was married, and they certainly did act like ladies. They did not utter one vulgar word. I asked Jennie if they got tipsy and she replied, "Only when they are blowing in the suckers for fizz at $5 a bottle."

I did not quite understand her, but remained silent and left. When I got outside and looked at the brightly lighted house with the piano music, and where all was life and gayety, and as I wandered in the dark to my room I thought, "Here are mistress and maid both alone in the west, one the rich owner of a house of pleasure and gayety and the mistress a homeless wanderer." Gazing at the stars above me I asked, "What shall I do for the best, and what will be my fate in these mighty mountains? Speak, and tell me, I pray thee."

CHAPTER VI.

ON inquiry I found out that I could not leave until the next day, as the stage had already gone, so I sat watching the strange people, when I saw all of them running to where two men stood with duck coats and leggins on and belts with cartridges and guns in their belts. As I turned to see what it was, the men pulled their guns and both seemed to fire at the same time. Both fell dead, and the ghastly look on their faces was terrible. Curley Frank was the name of the youngest, and he was a finely built and handsome man, with a fine education, and the son of a minister;the other was a finely built man. I learned by inquiry that he was at least ten years older than the other, and had a vicious look on his face. Though handsome, they were both faro dealers, and as the men fell there was a piercing shriek, and a small woman with red stockings on flung herself on the body of Curley Frank and sobbed bitterly. Some of the men pulled her away so the officers could take charge of the body. The woman was living with the man and was a dance hall girl. The officers hailed an express wagon and one grabbed a man by the collar and the other by the legs and threw them in the wagon as though they were logs of wood, and it was not more than fifteen minutes from the shooting till the music and the yelps of the gamblers were going on as if nothing had happened. I went into the place they called a hotel, which was a rough board building, and as there was no one in the waiting room I took the only rocking chair there was and sat by the window and thought this is what I have so many times wondered. What did become of doctors', lawyers' and ministers' children, for as a rule they live up to every cent they get, and have a servant to pin a napkin on them at the table, give them as good an education as they can, then put up their hands and say:

"Well, I have done well by my children, for I have given them a good education and brought them up to be good men or women," then turn them out on the world without a trade or a profession or a cent to start with and expect the girl to get a rich husband and the boys to get rich by their wits. Poor, foolish mothers! if they had beaten it into their brains that they had to get their own living and took them out of school in their teens and put them to whatever their own minds led to, what a different life they would live! For they read novels and wander out West, thinking they can find gold anywhere, and when they get there they find they can get nothing without money to pay for it, and that smart people have been there before them and have played every trick on the western people, as there is not a game thought of that has not already been played; then there is nothing left for them but gambling or playing tin horn or being kept by the red stockinged women, for they will not work and pay $1 for a cot to sleep on when there are three other women in the room.

Before I went to bed I took a walk up the street. There were tents instead of houses and I had not gotten very far when a man with a light broad-rimmed hat and a large, blood red silk handkerchief tied around his neck and a belt with cartridges and a big gun in it came up to me and said, "Well, when did you come to town?" I said:

"You are mistaken. You do not know me."

He said:

"We'll be westerners. It does not take long to get acquainted and you are just what I want, for you are a fairy, a beauty, by golly, and I can draw the crowd with a beauty like you in my dancehall, and I will do better by you than them other fellows, so come in here and I will set up a bottle of fiz on the strength of it."

I turned around quickly and began to walk rapidly towards the hotel. He kept up with me and we got in the front of a tent with music and a man yelling out the dance calls. He took hold of my hand and said:

"This is my place; come in."

I jerked away and answered:

"Keep your hands off of me or I will blow them off with this."

And I whipped out a .44. He stood as though he had been struck with lightning, and I went as fast as I could, without running, to the hotel. I had forgotten about my blonde hair and my fair skin, for it always attracted attention in London and in Paris. I was ashamed. As soon as I got to the hotel I went to my cot and tossed till near morning, for the mattress was hard hay, and lumpy, and it seemed I had only just fallen asleep when we were called up for the stage and had to start early. So I got a cup of coffee and two pancakes and was charged 75 cents for my breakfast, and as I stood on the porch waiting for the stage, the man with the red handkerchief came along with two other men, and as soon as he saw me he said to the men:

"That is the dry goods I was telling you about, with the fire of the sun, with the nerve of the merry devil in her, by golly."

Then the stage came up and I lost no time in getting in. There were three men and I in the four-horse stage when the driver cracked his whip and away we went. We had not gone very far when I found out that one of the men was from Alamosa and Alva Adams, hardware merchant, who was afterward Governor of Colorado and he had started a hardware store in Gunnison. His man had two very heavy satchels, and he said they were full of guns and cartridges.

The passengers were allowed fifty pounds of baggage and had to pay 10 cents per pound for all over that, and as I had two large trunks I was held up in good shape. We were in deep snow and it was near noon, but there was not a sign of any house where we could get a lunch, when one of the men said we should have brought a lunch with us, for it was after twelve o'clock now. I was nearly starving and it was after one o'clock when we saw a log place which looked like an old stable. The driver cracked his whip and stopped and three dirty little children came out and a dark, dirty looking man said dinner would be ready in ten minutes. When we went in there was fried ham, a dish of potatoes, a can of stewed tomatoes, dried apple pie, and such poor coffee, but we were all hungry and we had to pay 75 cents apiece. Then the driver came with fresh horses and a sleigh, and he told us we were going over the Cotton Wood Pass, and the dirty man said, "Yes, and you had better look after what you have of value, for yesterday's sleigh was held up. No one was killed, but they beat two men passengers up pretty badly."

And we had not got far when the man opened his satchel and took out three guns and loaded them, and said to the other two men:

"If anyone comes, you two grab one of them."

Then he turned to me and said:

"Do not get frightened at the sight of those guns, but we must be prepared."

I said:

"I came prepared," and took out a Smith & Wesson Blue Jacket double action .44. I said, "I will not be held up, and if you get one I will get two of them."

The men clapped their hands and said:

"You are a brick, and if they come at us they will catch a snag."

We were going up a hill all the way and the passes were white with snow, and it was getting late in the afternoon, when the driver said:

"I am afraid we cannot make it, for the horses are giving out."

I jumped over the seat to the front and said:

"Give me the lines and all of you get out and break the snow ahead of the horses," as it had been a heavy fall of snow all night and the road was blocked. It seemed as though the horses knew, for I gave them their own time and it took us two and one-half hours to get to the top of the summit, which was less than a mile, but when I saw the deep place we had to go down, I was very glad to let the driver take the lines, and I got back to my seat again, for it was getting dark and we were in heavy timber and snow, and could not see anything else. It was getting very cold. We kept on going for over three hours, and it was pitch dark when we saw a faint light ahead, and when we got to it it was a man swinging a lantern. He got in the sleigh and said:

"You are late. I thought those red devils had held you up as they did last night."

We soon got to a log cabin and it was clean, and we had a very nice supper with venison steak and nice hot biscuit. In one corner of the room was a bunk with a curtain all around it, and the woman said I was to sleep there, and as soon as the men went out I went to bed and slept soundly until daylight, and the next morning when the woman called me, I dressed on the bed behind the curtains, for the men had already come in the room to get warm, as it was very cold, and when I went to the door and looked out there was nothing but beautiful green trees and snow as far as I could see for miles in every direction.

Breakfast over, I asked for my bill, which was $3 for bed, supper and breakfast. We all got in the sleigh and away we went till noon, when the

Mrs. Captain Jack at Her Camp.

driver stopped at a log cabin. It was another driver. We had dinner there too rank to mention. Seventy-five cents was the price of it. The driver said we would have a tough time getting to Saquache that night, for the snow was so deep, and when we started the scenery was grand. The sun had melted some of the snow on the evergreens and it looked like thousands of diamonds as the sun rainbowed the icicles and they threw rays of every color. No one can imagine the wild beauty of these mountains, and the stillness added to the reverence I had for them. I had paid no attention to the conversation of the men until the driver said, "this is Noscuter Pass, and the snow that fell last night has blocked the road and we shall have to shovel a road:

I said:

"Give me the lines."

When I looked at the horses they were white with foam. There were only two shovels in the sleigh, so the others went ahead stamping the snow. It was getting very cold and the sun was beginning to get behind the mountains, when we heard a terrible screech. I said:

"What is that?"

The driver said:

"Wolves. Darn them, they think they are going to have a horse for supper tonight."

It seemed as though we never could go a mile. The men changed shoveling and it was dark. The wolves kept up their terrible howling and I thought I would freeze. Then the wind started up and blew a hurricane and blew the snow off the trees and all over us and the sleigh. The horses would go a few steps and then stop. Such a change in such a short time seemed almost impossible. It was pitch dark when we got to the top and the moaning of the wind, the noise of the timbers and the howling of the coyotes and wolves was something terrible.

The men got in and the driver took the lines, but the horses did not go fast, for the snow was too deep and it seemed we were hours in getting down the mountain. Then we had to go ten miles farther, but when we saw a light at a distance the men shouted with joy, and I was never so glad to see a little light in all my life.

We drove up to the adobe house where a lamp burning on the porch and the dogs began to bark till a little old man, German in his talk, said:

"Mine Got, it is near three o'clock. I thought you would not start after such a storm." The men said:

"Have you got any liquor? We are freezing."

He brought us a bottle and glasses and I took a big drink, for I was numb with the cold. There was a big stove in the room and it soon got hot. Then my feet began to burn. I tried to get my boots off, but couldn't, so had to get one of the men to cut them off, for my feet were swelling awfully and the pain was fierce. When the women came they said that my feet were frozen, and to take them away from the fire. They went and got something to put on them and wrapped them up. The pain made the tears roll down my cheeks. They got us a cold lunch and gave me a good bed, but in a cold room. I went to bed, but could not sleep with the pain in my feet.

When the stage was ready I could not go, for I could not get my boots on, and the store was not open, and my trunks were left behind for the freight wagons to bring. So when it got a little warmer I sent to the store for some shoes and got a pair two sizes larger than my own, but my feet were very sore and burnt. I went up the street and was surprised to see most of the people were Mexicans; all the houses were adobe, all the women wore shawls over their heads, and I noticed that some children and two women followed me. I went to the only store there was in town. They had everything in it, and after I had made a few purchases I said to the man:

"What are those people watching me for? Are they safe?" He laughed and said:

"They are as harmless as doves, but they have never seen such light hair nor anyone so fair, and they do not know what to make of it."

I went back to the hotel, went to bed and was awakened by shouts; it was near dark. I went to see about getting my supper when the landlady said: "The sleigh is in, for your sleigh broke the road for this outfit, and I miss my guess if there is not a devil of a time when the stage gets in Gunnison tomorrow, for there are two Pinkerton detectives on the sleigh and two came in with you last night."

I said, "What for?"

She said:

"There is a large reward for some of the boys in Gunnison and you bet they get them dead or alive."

And she turned to me and said:

"You must have grit to come on such a trip and all alone, for some of those dance-hall men would not stop at anything to get such a fair creature as you."

I said:

"I do not fear man or devil; it is not in my blood, and if they can shoot any straighter or quicker than I, let them try it, for a .44 equalizes frail woman and brute man, and all women ought to be able to protect themselves against such ruffians."

I got my supper and sat in the little parlor watching the people on the outside. All that I could see, for the town was not light and some of the men had come to get what news there was after the sleigh had come in, were two men smoking cigars and walking up and down the porch, and when the porch was cleared one of the men said:

"Yes, we must take no chances with the damned cop, for he is a dead shot and we must get the drop on him. But how about that other outfit? they are ahead of us. Well, we had better not know each other, we must be strangers and go around in different directions. Those dance-hall girls will be the best if there are any up there. So you look after them and I will see what comes to my net."

I went in and told the landlady to be sure to get me up in time to take the stage the next morning, and went to bed, as the sleighs went no farther. We had a new driver and a new stage the next morning when we started. It was a clear, cold morning and there were four men passengers. I took a look at them before I took my seat, and one rough young man, very fine looking, who looked like a cowboy, said:

"Here, miss, is a seat in the back, and those chaps in the front will break the wind off of you," as the stage was open and four horses in the front. So we started, but the detectives took different seats and sat with the driver. I was charmed with the scenery, and the young man tried to draw me out by inquiring if I had any friends in Gunnison, or what was my business, and it did not seem long until noon.

We stopped at a log cabin for dinner. The same old thing—ham, potatoes, tomatoes; 75 cents.

We had been on our way two hours or more. I said to the man:

"We will be in Gunnison tonight."

He said:

"Oh! no; we will not get further than Cochepota pass tonight, and it will not be daylight when we get there."

I found out that he was a cowboy, going to a large cattle ranch in Gunnison. He was very polite in his way, and told me many things of the West. It was now near dark. We met a man walking with a large bundle and a rope around his body. I said:

"Where has that man come from, and what has he on his back?"

He said:

"That is the way the mining men travel when they have their bedding on their backs and their hats on. They have all their possessions with them, and their home is wherever the night finds them. He has tramped from Siwatche and is making for the same stopping place we are; he is what we call a prospector; he goes and hunts mines and as soon as he finds a vein that shows up good, he will sell it for a few hundred, then the men who buy it sometimes make millions out of the mine. The men that find the mine very seldom get much out of it."

We went a few miles farther, then stopped at a log cabin for the night. They had a very nice supper, venison and nice hot biscuit, and as soon as supper was over I went to bed, for my feet burned so badly that I could hardly bear them. I did not go to sleep for a long time, and it seemed I had not been asleep long when I was wakened by a lot of men quarrelling, shouting and cursing; they kept it up till near daylight, and when I asked the woman the next morning what the men were quarrelling about, she looked at me and said:

"You must be a tenderfoot, or you would not ask such a question, for what would they quarrel over but a game of poker and too much booze?"

After breakfast I went outside to wait for the stage, and the first person I saw was the tramp who had been sleeping in the stable, and he was half drunk, for they sold whisky at this place.

The stage came in and I got in the back part, for they changed stages and drivers at every day's drive, and soon the cowboy came and sat beside me, and as he took his seat two men that came out of the barroom shook their fists at him and said:

Capt. Jack's First Camp, on the High Drive, Near Colorado Springs.

"Oh! we see why you would not drink liquor."

Then we started and heard no more, but by the conversation I learned that the cowboy won over $200 and he did not drink a drop of liquor.

We went sailing along till noon, then came to a two-story outbuilding which looked like a farm house, and as we stopped a lot of men came out and shouted, "Reaby or bust!"

This was Parlin; we had dinner there, and such fine mountain trout I never tasted. The fish were speckled trout, and harder, solider and sweeter fish never lived in water. All the talk was mines in Reaby, but they could not get at that for the snow, and as we were waiting for the stage a very handsome young man came and lifted his hat and said:

"I am afraid you will have a hard time to find a place to stop, for every place is so crowded with men waiting to get in Reaby." Then the cowboy said:

"I will see that she gets a place all O. K."

Then we started and went up a most beautiful valley overlooking a stream of clear, crystal, bubbling water; this was the Tomiche river, with sloping mountains on both sides of the valley, covered with all kinds of evergreen trees; the grass was green and full of wild flowers—such beauty of nature can never be told.

We went sailing along this valley till it was getting dark, when we came in sight of what looked like a military camp of tents, then the men shouted:

"Gunnison at last, by golly!"

We drove up to the only two-story building,

of rough green lumber, and not get finished. This was the Gunnison House, the only hotel in town, and as the stage stopped there were crowds of men who came to see who were on the stage, and nearly all had on buckskin suits, hats and belts with cartridges and guns in them, and cowboys' leather bands around their hats; nearly all seemed to have a mouthful of tobacco, and seemed to try who could chew the hardest, but they were a finely built, hardy looking set of men.

The cowboy turned to me and said:

"I will pass you off as a relation, as it will save you a great deal of annoyance. What is your name?"

I said:

"Ellen E. Jack, of New York."

He said:

"My name is Hall Greenleaf, but call me Hall, as I am known by that name."

He took me into the little waiting room and the landlady came in; then he said:

"This is a relation of mine, Mrs. Jack, and she wants to stay a day or two till she can look around."

The woman said:

"I have no place for ladies. Bull Pen is crowded both day and night, for the gamblers sleep in the daytime and the prospectors at night."

"Is there any place that I can get for her to sleep, and she can come here for her meals?"

"No, but I will let her sleep on this lounge for a night or two. It will be $1 a night."

"All right," I said, and took off my cloak.

She said:

"Put your satchel under the lounge, and if you have anything of value in it, take it out and hide it on yourself, as this is a very rough place."

I had diamonds and government bonds sewed up in my bustle and had nothing of value in the satchel. She brought me two old quilts and a dirty pillow with no case on it, and told me I had better not take all my clothes off, as the place was in such a state of excitement, and at nights it was the worst. So I loosened my corset, took off my shoes and garters and lay down, but not to sleep, for of all the noises, all night long, I never heard worse. Stamping up and down the stairs, throwing their heavy boots down on the uncovered floor, music going on on both sides of the house, and the gamblers yelling their games out, they being in tents, was as bad as being outdoors. I had heard of Bedlam, but this beat that place.

At daylight she opened the inner door and told me to get up, as she had to use that room for offices as well as waiting room, so I was soon ready to let the people in the office, but I had to wait till near nine o'clock before I could get my breakfast. Then I went out to see the town. I went back of the hotel, where there were some small tents, thinking I might rent one till I knew what I was going to do, and as I got near the second one I stood still, uncertain in which one to go, and turning around to go to the first, a gun shot bore a hole through my cloak and two more shots went close by me and into the tent. Then a man came out in his drawers and shirt, with gun in hand, and he was covered with blood. He gave me such a piercing look that I fired. Then there was a volley of shots. The man fell and the two detectives ran to him and said:

"Damn you, we have got you at last."

The dying man said:

"You have used a fair decoy to catch me."

The two men said:

"No, but we guess she was coming to give you the tip."

I said:

"You are both mistaken. The landlady at the hotel told me I might rent one of these tents. That was what brought me here, and now you have got this poor unfortunate man. Do not hurt him any more. For he is a dying man."

I went up to him, for I could see the two men were afraid to go nearer as long as he had life and a gun in his hands.

I said:

"Give me your gun."

He nodded his head, and as I stooped to take it he tried to tell me something. By this time there were crowds of men and they shouted, "They have got Wild Bill!" and "Where did he get that fair gal from?" But as soon as I had his gun in my hand the two men came up and said:

"We hold you as witness that we got him first."

The poor man was not quite dead and I was still on my knees, stroking his head and face, when he opened his eyes so pitiful.

I said:

"Father in heaven, forgive him, for we know not what hardship drove him to commit the misdeeds that have caused his death."

He tried to speak, but gave a shiver, closed his eyes and was dead.

I got up with the gun in my hand. One of the men said:

"Give me that gun."

I said:

"No. He gave me the gun, for you were too big a coward to get it, and you shall never have it."

When I turned to go, Hall was close to me and he shouted:

"The gun was a dying gift to this lady and it is hers. What say you, boys."

All shouted:

"The man who tries to take it shall pass in his chips quicker than Bill did."

These two men had watched him all night and had waited till they were sure he was asleep and when they saw me going and were uncertain about the tent, they thought I was going to warn him of them. Then they began to fire in the tent, for they knew just where he slept, and they shot him in the back, and another bullet struck the side of his head, and that was what covered him with blood.

Hall took my arm and we got out of the crowd and went off the main street when he said:

"I have been looking out for you and found a large tent and cook stove that were brought here for a dance hall, but the man lost all the money he had a few nights ago bucking the tiger. He wants $225 for both. The tent, which is 24x50, has six small rooms partitioned off for bedrooms for the girls, but it has never been put up, as there is no lumber in town, but he ordered the lumber for the frame last week and it may come in any day. That would be extra."

So we went to the corral to see the man and tent. The stove was a large Charter Oak cooking stove, so I offered him $200 for both and got them. Then we went to see about lots, and I bought a lot close to the main street and had the first log cabin on it that was built in Gunnison. I paid $400 cash down for it to to Mr. Harlowe, who had just put up a tent and his wife was keeping a restaurant and could not accommodate a quarter of the people at 50 cents a meal. Mrs. Harlowe took me to a woman who had a small tent, and I got a cot to sleep on at 50 cents a night till the lumber came. I had to wait for ten days and when it did come it was wet, green lumber and at $90 a thousand. It had to be hauled by wagons from Lake City, and as the spring was breaking there was mud up to the hubs in places. When the carpenters came to put it up they charged $8 a day, so I got the tent up without a floor, just the frame. Then I had to buy a long, rough lumber table and six three-legged stools, all by the pound. There were a few cots in town. I paid $12 for one single cot; and I had not gotten my trunks yet. I went every day to see about them, for I had some table linen and some silverware in them, but as soon as the tent was up and the stove in place I went to housekeeping with a tin plate and a tin cup, and a soap box for a table and another for a seat, whilst I was waiting for the table and stools. When I had been in Gunnison fifteen days my trunks came and I had to pay $40 before they would give them to me, for they had charged 10 cents a pound and had charged it at every new sleigh or stage. Each one had charged the 10 cents, then had sent them through by the freighters; such stealing I could not imagine. I thought they were taking advantage of me and playing me for a tenderfoot, as they called all Eastern people, but as I inquired I found out I ought to have sent my baggage by the freight teams, then it would have been 10 cents through, but as I did not know I fell in the stage graft or express graft. They pretended to send it by express, when it came by freight. My table and three-legged stools cost me over $30, so I opened a restaurant and called it "Jack's Cabin." I put the tent by the log cabin, and the teamsters came to it the first place, where they washed themselves. I paid $1.50 a barrel for water. A half-Mexican, called "Daby John," and two other men sold water and I bought half a ton of coal for $10.

The Jews were coming by every stage and brought big tents of every kind with freight loads. They brought all kinds of merchandise to sell and the prospectors were trying to get to the mining camps. A great many of them were killed by snow-slides and when I had them near two months a freighter came and brought me about a dozen red apples and a small cabbage which was $1.50. I left them on the table, as they were a great treat. I heard such a noise that I went down to the front; the tent was full of Indians. They had stolen my apples and were scrambling to see which should get them, and the one that did get one would give a bite to the other who had none, but he held fast to the apple while the other took a bite, and of all the sights—they had moccasins and "brichants" and red blankets over their shoulders, their bodies and arms were covered with hair, their faces were all covered with paint, and their long, coarse, black hair, with bits of every-colored dirty rags, yellow rags tied around little strips of hair, and necklaces of chestnuts.

I stood looking on when they all came around me, and one big buck, who had large gold earrings, came to me dancing and trying to touch my hair. I thought they wanted to scalp me to get my light hair, and as they began to get closer a man called out at the door to me and said:

"Stand your ground and have no fear, for they have gotten some fire-water and there is no telling what they may do."

He talked to them in their own language. Then he said to me:

"'Colorou, their medicine man, wants to feel your hair, so let him.

I took his hand and put it on my head and let my mass of yellow hair down, and they all danced around me and touched my hair; then jumped away as though they had been stung by a bee, but Colorou wanted a little of it, so I backed to the kitchen and got a pair of scissors and cut off a good size lock of it and went up to Collarow and pinned it on his blanket. He was delighted with it. He stroked and patted it as though it had life in it. The man was their interpreter and had charge of them. He got them away and I was glad, for I was a great favorite of the freighters, and I expected a lot of them in that night and had to get ready for their supper. They were paying $10 for a man to carry a five-gallon keg of whisky two miles on snow shoes up to Reuly, and the snow was going fast, but there was great danger of slides. A lot had gone up to Crested Butte and some to Reuly, but everything had to come to Gunnison first, and rough buildings were going up fast. Then a dance hall came, a large tent, and they called it "The Lady Gay." It was not very far from me, so I heard all day the noise of their caller roaring out their dances. There were saw-mills coming in the surrounding timber near town, so the town was building fast. I got a floor, a front door and windows, some chairs and more tables, and a man cook, for there were not many women in town that would work. Some men brought their wives with them to take up ranches as soon as the Ute Indians were taken off their reservation. I was doing a good business when the fall came and what they called "mountain fever" set in. There was a Dr. Woods who built a drug store and had a room in the back of it, and a bank; the cashier, Sam Gill, and his wife lived in the back of the bank. It had a good safe in it and seemed to do good business there. There was a Dr. Mitchell who came from Denver and bought the corner of my property and made a contract for a large two-story stone building; stores downstairs and rooms upstairs. He was a tall, fine-looking handsome man. He came to me and said:

"I feel badly. I am afraid I am going to be sick."

I said:

"Go and lie down on the cook's bed and when the rush is over I will make you a cup of strong tea."

He went and laid down about half an hour and then came and got his tea, but could not eat anything. He started to go across the street and fell. I ran to him and raised his head.

He said:

"Oh! my wife, my wife!"

I yelled for help and some one brought a cart and put him in it and took him to Dr. Woods, but when they took him in the back room he died. It was mountain fever; he had it for several days, but neglected it.

One day some men came and asked me if I had an old boiled shirt, as a man had died and they wanted to put a white shirt on him to be buried in and there were no prayer books in town. I said:

"I have no shirt, but I have a prayer book, both Catholic and Protestant, and a hymn book."

They said:

"That's the stuff. We can send him off decently, but who knows about reading that funeral business?"

I said:

"Why, Old Man Braun, who has a landlady in the tent back of the Gunnison House," so off they went with my book and got Braun to read the funeral or something over the man.

Two days later two women came to borrow my hymn books, as Maud Kelly, a little girl had died of the mountain fever, was left $30,000 by Colonel Hall. They asked me to go and help sing a hymn over her. I went. It was in the front of my place. They had turned an old blacksmith shop into a church and had got Old Man Braun to read the services over her, and we sang two hymns; all the women there were on the ranches came in to the funeral. Mr. Kelly, her father, was one of the first county commissioners and a ranchman. He came riding in to town and would stop in front of Sallow's and call for drinks for everyone that was near, and after he had drank he would throw his glasses to the ground and break them, then throw a five or ten-dollar bill to the man and tell him to take the damage out of it, and when he came in town he would whoop and yell like an Indian and keep it up, going from one saloon to another and throwing money away, but when his term of office was out the taxpayers found out they had to pay for all of that.

CHAPTER VII.

MY business was increasing so that I had to buy more lots and buildings. I had just finished building No. 2 when the handsome man I first saw at Parlin, and whose name was Jeff Mickey, arrived. He was the only son of a wealthy banker from Shelby, and was a very highly educated man. He spoke four languages and was an all-around sport. He came to me one day and wanted to rent my building No. 2 for a saloon. I did not like that, but it seemed to me that the best people in town were saloon people or faro dealers, so I rented him building No. 2, but on the condition that there should be no gambling allowed in the place.

I was taking a great interest in mining and got the prospectors to bring me specimens of mineral and explain all about the veins and formations, and in the meantime Jeff Mickey had gotten his place fitted up and had started. He drew crowds, for he was well liked and had a bunk house put up like the sleeping cars, one bunk above the other, so that I could accommodate one hundred men at 50 cents a night. I was buying all the lots adjoining my place that I could get, for "Jack's Cabin" was headquarters for the freighters and it was very crowded at nights, when there was a great deal of excitement in town and the sheriff and posse all took horses and went tearing past my place, for we learned that the Indians were getting ready to waylay the freighters and rob them. There was a freighter with his nephew, named Jackson, who was camping for the night, and an Indian went to get something to eat; the man told him to get out, when he pulled a sheath knife to kill the man. The boy, seeing his game, pulled his gun and killed the Indian, and as soon as the Indians learned of it they wanted to kill all the whites. The sheriff went to get young Jackson, and they brought him in and put him in a calaboose, the only place there was then, but as the crime was committed on a reservation the civil attorneys had no jurisdiction over it, so Cline, the Indian agent, came for him. The officers at the fort wanted to send a military guard with him, but he said he knew a trail that could bring him safe and not arouse the Indians, so the sheriff turned him over to Cline. Two days after the word came that Cline had formed a conspiracy with the chief and Collarow, and he had them meet him and take the boy. Cline made a lot of money off of the Indians. He sold them tobacco and all sorts of things and was getting rich off of them. He did not want to be an enemy to them. They gave the boy to the squaws to torture him to death and they tore his tongue out with fish hooks and put his eyes out with red hot wire, and every time he shrieked they danced around him and laughed with glee. The crime was committed twenty-four miles out of Gunnison, and that was on the reservation, but Gunnison City was not on the reservation, but was a county seat and incorporated, and that made Cline responsible to the Gunnison authorities, so they went and got him and put him in a calaboose, but the freighters got wind of it and took their wagons and left their horses and rode to town to hang Cline. They had made it up for Bud Miller to throw a rock through a gamblers' window and get arrested, and if Cline was there, he should light a match and hold it to the window. Then they would tear the door down and bring a rope and hang him, but the sheriff got wind of what they were up to and took him out and hid him in an old cabin with two guards over him. The freighters were in the greatest excitement for over an hour and no light could be seen. They went and paid Bud's fine and took him out. There were over one hundred freighters at "Jack's Cabin." and such a night I put in! I never went to bed. The next day was nearly as bad, for they thought the Utes would come and take the town. But the third day the freighters went back after their wagons and we thought it was all over, when the Utes came at night and started to take the town, with some outlawed whites. The Frenchmen would go in a place first and see how the land lay, then start a fight and the small band of Indians would rush in and do their work. They cleaned the Gunnison houses out, then came to "Jack's Cabin," as it was the freighters' quarters, and started the fight there, but Jeff was a powerful man and quick. He fought like a demon, but there were too many for him. They got out doors and all the men went outside. It was so quick. Some of the lamps had been knocked down and the oil had caught fire on the board floor and was setting fire to the buildings. I tore my apron off and dipped it in water and began to beat the fire out when I was struck on the forehead with a tomahawk. I jumped back and grabbed my two guns and went to the door and began to fire. I fell on my knees from loss of blood, but I emptied my guns while I was kneeling. The shooting brought nearly all the town to the cabin. The Indians, seeing such a crowd, sneaked off in the dark, but a lot of them lay dead all around the place; two of the Frenchmen were known and the officers got them into express wagons and threw the dead men in, and I never knew what they did with them. They were afraid all of the Utes would swarm Gunnison, and if they did they would kill every one before the troops could save them. They carried five wounded men in and said that Jeff was dead.

The doctors came and found my skull was broken in, and I was in a very dangerous condition. Jeff was not dead, but badly cut and wounded. They sewed up my wound, but I went out of my head. The next day the interpreter came and seeing the condition I was in said:

"Colorou is the only one that can save the woman, for the thing she was struck with was poison."

Late in the afternoon Colorou went into a restaurant, took hold of a white tablecloth, threw all the dishes on the floor and got on his pony, waving the white flag of truce. The people all yelled.

"The Indians are coming on the war path!"

Every man jumped to his gun or anything he could find, but seeing no one but the chief, they waited and watched. He came to "Jack's Cabin" and showed my hair on his blanket, and yelled:

"Pale face! me wants to save her."

So they brought him to me. He did not know how to get the bandage off of my head, so they sent for my doctor. He took it off and Colorou said:

"Bloody poison killy the white squaw, and we lovey the pale face."

He stroked my hair on his blanket and said:

"Me will killy the brave that struck the pale face."

He took something from a pouch and laid it on my head and gave me a pill as big as a bullet. He left some more for me to take every hour, and said he would come next day.

He took the tablecloth and when he got to the restaurant he threw it on the door and went off to his wigwam. I wandered away and thought I was on top of a very high mountain which was covered with snow, and I would cry out:

"Jenny, where are you? My little Jenny is not in the place I left her."

When I went to go farther a man came to me and said:

"What are you seeking?"

I said:

"My little child. They took all I had but one, and now I have lost her."

"Not so.

"You are going west and she is in the east; come, thou brave, wanderer of earth, and I will guide thee."

And as I took his hand to go I looked at him and cried out:

" 'Tis my beloved husband. Why do you not take me to your home? I am so tired of this desolate place, with not one of kin or one whom I can confide in. Oh! take me, take me, I pray you."

He said: "Nay, I cannot take you, for you were born to go through what you are going through now, and your sorrows and trials will live after you are with me. When your work is done on this earth plane, come; we will go to our child," and it seemed we went sailing through air to New York and to the Queninbosh mansion in Eighteenth street and up on the top floor. I stood at the foot of a bed and there lay my Jenny, and as I looked at her she was crying and said:

"Oh! why did my mother leave me here all alone?" and the tears rolled down her cheeks.

I went to her and kissed her tear-stained face and petted her. Then my husband said:

"Come, we must go."

And we sailed away to the West again and went to the room where my body lay as though in death. It seemed as though all was dark, and then I came to my senses again and there sat on the foot of my bed the Cave boy all in tears, for they thought I was dying and had sent for the doctor. He came and ordered stimulants and beef tea for me and said that I was too faint to drink, so they gave me wine. When the gamblers found it out they went around to the back doors of the restaurant and gave big tips to the cooks, so as to get them to make nice things and beef tea for me, for it was very hard to get anything nice in such a rush, and my place was closed, for the cooks ran away, afraid of Indians, and two others of the help were wounded and in bed. I was helpless. When the poor unfortunate girls brought nice things to me I was thankful. Several days after Collarow had put his leaves on my head, two sticks broke loose and a lot of black blood and water came from the wound, and when Collarow came he said:

"Paleface will get better; bad blood come," and the weather was getting bitter cold. The men got up and went out to their meals.

I was as helpless as a child.

A family had come to town with two girls and I got one of them to come two hours in the morning and two in the afternoon, for $10 a week. It was Christmas now; Jeff had been well some weeks, but I had just begun to sit up, and Collarow wanted to come and smoke his pipe and sit in the kitchen. I was the worst looking thing. I was fainter when I saw myself in the glass. The green flood had settled all down my face, and the scar was a sight. I had to keep my head bandanged all winter, for if the frost had gotten to it there is no telling what would have become of poor me.

The people kept coming and I had to open. One week the surveyors came to survey for the D. & R. G. railroad and my place was crowded. I bought more lots and put up more buildings, and in the spring the government moved the Indians. The United States district attorney came and made the Gunnison attorneys give Cline up to the fort, so the soldiers came and took him to the fort a prisoner and I promised when I was better I would go and see Collarow in his new home. He was very sad at leaving and became "silverished." He gave me a pretty pouch of pills and a lot of herbs and told me what they were to cure. Then he took my hands and stroked them and said:

"Bye, bye."

Then he made a run for the door as if he did not want me to see the tears in his eyes, and that was the last time I ever saw him.

The surveyors made "Jack's Cabin" their home and they were a gay set of men; one, a tall middle-aged man, named Hank, borrowed a woman's mother hubbard wrapper and put it on. It came to his knees and he tied a large apron around his waist and had a woman's hat and parasol; he went up Main street in that rig and all the gamblers and men would come out and whoop and yell, but he never laughed, not a smile, and when they were getting ready to move, one of their men got hurt and there was not a place in town to take a sick man to, so I let him have one of the little rooms and got a doctor, and at night I put two bottles of hot water wrapped up in some flannel, in bed with him. It was very cold. A blizzard was blowing and I put a large lump of coal down before I went to bed, but in the night I was awakened by the yelling. I am boosted up and I am boosted up. I got a light and my red blankets were white with frost all around where my breath had gone on them, and my ear was frozen stiff in the front. I got some clothes on and went to Ike and he said:

"I am freezing. Those damned bottles are busted."

I took the covers off his feet and sure enough the hot water bottles were "busted" and ice all over the bed clothes.

I took them out and wrapped them up in my petticoat and went to look at the fire. It had gone out. I made a fire and put on a lot of coal and got to bed again, but my head pained me so I could not sleep. I covered my head up under the bed clothes. Early in the morning the cook brought me something he called a cocktail; he said Mr. Jeff had sent it and that everything was frozen; the barometer had stopped at 42 degrees below zero and he had given the sick man a drink the same as mine. The men began to come in and the whole town was frozen up. I had a well sunk fifty-two feet deep and it was frozen on the top. The boys had to put large rocks in the buckets and break the ice before they could get any water. There were people of all classes coming to town, and among them was a young attorney, Frank A. Gaudey and Ike Stevens, a tall, slim young man. A lot of dead-beats came to "Jack's Cabin" to give me a stand off. Ike was up and had a little shawl over his head; the doctor had painted his face with iodine, as he had erysipelas in his head and face. I said to them, as they came in:

"If you are afraid of the smallpox, do not come in here."

Ike turned and looked at them with his painted face and the shawl over his head. He looked a fright. They stood for a minute or two and then went as if they had seen a ghost. So I got rid of the dead-beats and Ike soon got well and went to the surveyors' gang again.

A few weeks after this I was very busy when one of the help came to me and said:

"There will be trouble in the bunkhouse, for Jim is full and has a gun, and is abusing one of the carpenters."

I said:

"Well, go and throw him out."

He said:

"Not me, by gosh; I don't want to be killed by that drunken whelp."

I went in my room, and took my gun and went to the bunkhouse and said:

"What are you growling about? Get out of this."

He said:

"Not till I have settled with this son of a b——" and pulled his gun to fire at the man. I pulled mine and shot the gun out of his hands and part of his hand off with it.

I said:

"Now go, or I will wing off the other hand."

He began to yell, but got afraid I would give him another shot, so he went, and as soon as he had gone the carpenter said:

"Words are empty, for you have saved my life and I have a wife and two children depending on me for a living."

I said:

"What was the trouble?"

He said:

"Jim wanted to borrow $5 of me and I told him I did not have it. Then he began his abuse, and I am afraid he will do something yet, for the very old Satan is in that lad."

I said:

"No, he is a coward, for he knew that he had the drop on you; that you were unarmed, but he did not think of me being so quick and taking such a straight shot. He will never try to come at me."

That night the officers told me I was under arrest, so I went and got Frank Gowdy and gave a bond for $1,000, and I would not let the justice try the case, but took it to the county court, before Judge Smith. When the trial came off we all went to court and the jury was all sworn in. The man had Ike Stevens, and both the young attorneys began their case and all at once Stevens called Gowdy a liar, and as soon as he had Gowdy struck him a paster on the nose and blood was streaming down his face; when they both began to fight all the jurors jumped from their seats and got to scrapping, and old Judge Smith jumped upon his desk and yelled out:

"I fine you both for contempt of court." Then some one struck him with a chair and knocked him off of the desk. The sheriff tried to grab some one when old Jack Seamon struck him and sent him head foremost over some chairs; they were fastened together, and when I saw him go over, his coat-tails opened behind and his ears sticking up as he went on all-fours over the back of the chairs, I thought I would die laughing. But as soon as the men got out of the fight they made for the door and out. I never heard anyone say court adjourned or any more about fining for contempt, nor was anyone arrested, but all got out as fast as they could, and when I got on the main street three old dead-beats that I had fired out of my place stood on the corner. I was laughing at the sight, it was so comical, but those men saw the bloody handkerchief and black eyes of two of the men, then saw me laughing. One of them said:

"There, I told you she had done it."

Just then Frank McMaster, who had just got a little newspaper, came up to the men and said:

"What's up?"

The man, who did not know anything only what he had surmised, said:

"Why, that yellow-haired girl has cleaned the court room up with a gun and licked both judge and jurors, and then turned loose on both lawyers and sheriff. They all have bloody faces and one a black eye, and the poor old judge is getting his wrist set, as she must have broken it with the butt end of her gun."

The newsman went back to his office with all

this, and as it was press time he put it all in the paper, with big headings of "Mrs. Captain Jack, the Dare Devil of the West," had cleaned the county court room out, and a lot more that the man told him, when the truth was that I was the only one that was not in the fight. The only part I took was to laugh at George Hues, the sheriff, going over the chair backs.

Well, that paper went to Denver, then all the papers in the United States of America had me as one of the worst and most daring women that had ever lived. It seemed that every paper added a little more to it. They even sent agents from New York to get a picture of me to put in the *Police Gazette*, and all this was through the vicious tongue of old man Kirkbe.

My trial did not come up for several weeks after, and when it did I was fined $15 and costs for saving a man's life and at least $1,000 expense to the county for prosecuting the murderer, but the game was to get what they could out of me, and they knew if they made the fine too large I would carry the case up. I was very angry at being fined, but paid it, and a few weeks after Judge Smith came to me to see about some land I had gotten, and after he got through with the land business he said:

"You see if you had not shot that man I would not have gotten my wrist sprained, and it gives me a great deal of pain and trouble."

I said:

"Is that why you fined me for saving a good man's life and disarming a ruffian?"

He said:

Captain Jack—Mining Queen

"Well, no, not that."

I said:

"Judge, you ought to have been in your grave ten years ago. You are not fit to judge between right and wrong. You remind me of a piece of old parchment that has done its work, and when election day comes I will do mine. I cannot vote but I can get the boys to vote for me."

And when election came there were stickers with names on, and we cut off the name we wanted and stuck it over the name we did not want. I was very busy fixing up my tickets and getting the boys to vote them, and the Judge got beat. He started to sell out everything he had, and got his wife to help him, and when he had gotten all he could he took the only child of a widow, seventeen years old, and disappeared and left his poor old wife and daughter without home or money. That is a sample of the officers we had in those days.

The town was still booming and there was a man who had been an officer for many years in causes, whose name was Jimmy McClease. Jeff knew him for many years, so I got him on the police force. The town was very rough; four dance halls and a variety of theaters and a lot of other bad places. It was nothing to find men dead in alleys and robbed, and the authorities did not try to find out who committed the crimes, for there was not money enough in the treasury to prosecute half of them.

Then the graders of the D. & R. G. railroad came and another set of surveyors for the South Park railway. The coal mines that had been opened up were making still more excitement. I took up two coal mines and put four men to open them up, but sold them for $1,000, as I could not look after them. Jeff Mickey was drinking and running with sporty women, and I did not like that. It kept me on nettles all the time, with fear that something would happen; and Buffalo Bill Cody, the show man that is now, was known as Bill Specte then. He used to bring me mountain species of sheep which were fine, and he brought me a lot of fox skins, enough to make a carriage robe. He was known as a scout and an Indian interpreter, and was an all-round good fellow. There was a man named Cal Mace who had fitted up the handsomest gambling saloon in town, and Jamey McClease told me that he was the most dangerous man that ever came to town, for a reward of over $5,000 was hanging over him for killing two men in Texas. It was not many nights after, I was told, that there was a crowd running to the Yard's dance hall, which was just opposite my place, and there was Jimmie sleeping in his room. I went to his door and said:

"Get up, Jim; there is a row over the way.'

He was soon up out of his room and when he was half way across the street he turned back and said:

"Lend me your gun. I have left mine in my overcoat pocket."

I loaned him the very gun that I had shot the hand off with. He went into the dance hall and found out that Cal Mace's bartender was on a drunk and had beaten one of the girls over the head with a bottle; he had cut her shamefully and the men were trying to put him out. As Yard was not in and he had pulled a gun on them, Jem got him out and took him to his room and told him to go to bed or he would get into trouble.

I had a little hunchbacked woman who worked for me and slept with me because rooms brought too much money to give her an extra room. About nine o'clock she went to bed and as all was quiet I went to bed about ten, but before I went I loaded my other gun and put it under my pillow. We had been in bed some time and was sound asleep when some one burst in my door, and as I reached for my gun the man said:

"Hold, it is I, Jim."

I said:

"How dare you break into my room?"

He said:

"Get a light, quick, for I am shot, but I had to kill him."

I said to Anna:

"Get up and go to Jeff's room and tell him to get up."

She said:

"He is not in his room."

Jim had a large army gun and his hands were streaming with blood:

I said:

"I thought the man had gone to bed."

Jim said:

"He got up and began his fighting again and I took him to Cal's saloon, when Cal said, 'I know what you are after,' meaning the reward, and he pulled his big gun and shot through Jim's finger, but before he could fire again Jim fired three shots just as quick. My gun was self-cocker, double action, and killed him."

After he fell Jim took the gun away from him and brought it to his room.

I said:

"You had better get a doctor to see how much you are hurt."

He said:

"Stop the flow of blood, for I am feeling faint."

I bandaged his finger and hand the best I could, then he went to get Dr. Rockerfellow and give himself up to the sheriff, but there was no more sleep for us that night. The next morning as soon as the saloon men and gamblers heard of Cal's being killed by Jim McClease, an officer, they were furious and made threats of lynching him, for they heard nothing of the reward or his crimes, and there was a sporting woman, who kept the largest sporting house in town, whose name was Molly Keese, and she had this man for a lover. She got on a drunk and at night she gathered a band of tin horns and all-round bad men that were broke and offered them $500 to take Jim out and hang him. There were mobs gathering to go to the jail for Jim. Then the sheriff found out what was doing. He sent to me to have all the trusty men I could get, and as soon as I could, for he had not force enough, and I had a hundred men boarding at "Jack's Cabin." When I had thirty-six men ready they said:

"By gosh, the sheriff might shoot at us and think we belonged to the other side."

I said:

"I will go first."

So I went a few yards ahead of them and went up the steps to the jail and called out:

"Captain Jack is here; open the door."

They had a chain on the door and opened it just enough to peek through, I said:

"I have a band of good trusty men; let them in. I was afraid you might mistake them for the other side if I had not come in with them."

He said:

"Get them in, quick." I hopped up and they all came running up the steps and the sheriff swore them all in as deputies.

Not a minute too quick, for the mobs were coming in from three different directions. I said:

"Let me out before they get here."

He said:

"They will see you and get you sure."

I said:

"Let me out of the back door and put out all the lights. I will go on all fours till I get far enough away."

So I went as fast as I could to my own back door, for I knew my place had been watched, and I sent over to the dance hall to tell Mr. Yard to come to me at once. He came and I told him about the reward, and that was why Cal wished a very different light on it, and I asked him to keep a sharp lookout for my place, as they might try to blow it up with dynamite. Yard said he would go to the saloon, which was next door to his place on the corner and kept by George Welsh and Tom Creeal, both Texans. As soon as they found out that this was the man that was wanted for the two murders in Texas they went to all the saloons and told why Jim had to kill him or be killed himself, and as soon as the truth was known they let up on their cry to hang him and would have nothing to do with it, but the women had gotten a lot of tin-horns drunk enough to do anything and they went to the jail and yelled out that they wanted Jim McClease, and were met with a volley of shots. The sheriff told the men to fire over the men's heads as a warning, and then the mob yelled and cursed and made threats. The sheriff opened a window and told the mob to go away or he would fire to kill and that he had force enough to take care of his prisoners. They expected the saloon men to come and help them and were waiting for a leader to make the break, when three men came to the mob and said:

"We fear the jig is all up, for every one of the faro dealers and the saloon men have gone back on us, as they have found out something about Cal Hays, and say he only got what he ought to get; that he was going to be married to this Molly Keese when he had a wife and two children who came to Gunnison when they heard of the death, and as soon as the woman heard for sure that he was a married man she said if Jim had not killed him she would, for it was all her money that had fitted up the gambling saloon. Over $3,000 had gone, but she took all the things and the gamblers made up a purse for the widow to go back to Texas.

Jeff and another man came to me to get me to go on Jim's bond, which was $50,000. I would not go on it, for I was getting sick of such work and all the outfit. It made Jim very angry, for he had banked on me, so he had to stay in jail, and when he had been in between three and four weeks he all at once disappeared, and there was a great outcry about it. I knew nothing about it, but I knew that Jeff avoided me, and that he and a man called Sailor Jack, that worked around the kitchen, were up to something that was not straight, and I mistrusted them. Jim had been missing about ten days and every place had been searched that a likely place for him to be in, when one Sunday the sheriff deputized fifty men to come to my place. I saw them coming down the street and said to Annie:

"I wonder what the trouble is," and Sailor Jack jumped up and went in the barroom to Jeff. They stopped in front first and then surrounded the place. The sheriff came in and said:

"We want Jim McClease."

I was indignant and said:

"You are welcome to him if you can find him."

There were five buildings adjoining each other and it was not a very easy thing to find anyone if we did not want them found, and as I stood in the dining room Mr. Burten, the hardware merchant, came to me and said:

"It will save trouble to give him up, for it is known for sure that he is in this place."

Then all at once I thought of Jack, I beckoned to the sheriff and said:

"Are you sure he is here?"

He said:

"Yes."

I said:

"I want to go in my room and get my gun, then I will find out the truth of it and where he is and will get him for you."

He said:

"I do not want you to get a gun."

I said:

"Then I will not help."

Burten said:

"Are you sure you do not want to use the gun on the deputies?"

I said:

"On my word as a woman I will not turn the gun on the deputies."

They both went with me to get the gun. I went to the kitchen and said to Sailor Jack:

"Where is Jim's hiding place."

He said:

"I don't know."

I struck him over the face with the gun and said:

"Show me quick or I will fix you."

He went to his room and fainted on the floor. Then I knew but had forgotten a small cellar that we dug to keep potatoes from freezing, before the large cellar in building No. 2 was built. I pulled up a board and said:

"Jim, the jig is all up. You have to come up and give yourself up, for the place is surrounded with deputies."

He said:

"I will surrender to you, but not to them."

I went to the sheriff and said:

"Bring all your men in the front, for he will surrender to me, but not to you. I will get his gun away from him, then turn him over to you."

So I went back and said:

"Come out of that; I am waiting for you."

He came out and when he was in the room I said:

"Give me the gun. You do not want it."

He did not want to give it up, but I said:

"You must keep your peace with me and surrender that gun and yourself to me."

He handed the gun to me.

I said:

"Come, there is nothing left here but to go back with them. It would be death to attempt to escape."

So he walked with me to the No. 2 dining room where the sheriff was.

I said:

"Here is your prisoner, sir, and you take care of him. It is your business to take care of him, not mine."

So they all surrounded him and marched to the jail that night.

A Jewish merchant named Bail came to me and said:

"See, now, those cursed churches are coming in town, there will be no more luck or peace, for they stick their noses into everybody's business to get money and play that they are doing some good. One of them came to Burten and me, and said:

"I will swear out a warrant for you for harboring a murderer."

"We told him he had better mind his own business; that we got along very well before his outfit came and we were here first and you gave them $50 to build that church. You will see what they will give you for it."

That is one thing you must admit. The Jews never interfere with anyone's church or business, and when I turned back to look at the Jews I had met in London and Paris, I never remembered about a remark about our churches, and never heard of one of them trying to get a convert.

But the other churches are doing all they can to get converts and are preaching that they are following the workings and teachings of the Jesus Christ.

I say:

It is false. They do not follow after his teachings, for he cast out evil spirits and cured the sick and said: "As I do ye shall do also," and greater things also, and until these ministers come down off their pulpits and cast out devils or evil spirits out of the congregation and cure the sick, they are not what they claim to be. Go into the church and look at the congregation, all well dressed people and gray-haired old women and bald-headed old men. They pray to Almighty God to send them prosperity. He has already sent them poor brothers who have to have money at 2 per cent per month, or as much more as they can hold them up for, and practice usury from Monday morning to Saturday night; then Sunday morning their piety starts and ends Sunday night, and they have done their duty. They have thanked God for sending the poor creatures at 2 per cent a month, and asked him to send them some more through the week till Sunday comes again. I know a preacher who had a son at college, and it was his last term, and when the boy came home his father took him by himself and said:

"My son, you must choose a profession for yourself, now that you are out of college."

The boy said:

"Well, you wear good clothes and have everything that is good and a lot of women paying you compliments and making a pet of you all the time. What if I should follow suit and be a minister and have an easy time of it too?"

And yet there is something in the churches and Sabbath schools that is beautiful. I can look back to childhood days when I went to Sunday school, and very often in my rambles through the mountains I offered up a prayer for my teachers, whom have long ago passed from this beautiful shore. The path the ministers are taking is by far too narrow; they must widen with the age of progression.

Monday at noon I was arrested. The policeman swore out a warrant for me, but Mickey McClease had not been convicted of murder, so I could not harbor one till the law said he was one.

I went up the street and asked the merchants to go on my bond. There were five of them there in five minutes after we got to court. Two of them signed, but the judge would not let the others sign the bond, for two was enough, so the other three were quite slighted, but they all held a meeting at four o'clock in the afternoon and the news spread like wild fire, and that night a crowd of men went to the policeman's house and woke him up. They took him to the end of the town and gave him a good sound thrashing and told him to get away from town as fast as he could, for if he ever came back he would never get a chance to go again, for they would hang him till he was dead.

They had a paper already signed saying:

"Go on with your church, and the one that interferes with the other's business will go as quick as the one that has just gone." They tacked this paper on his door, and that stopped their interference for a while.

They begged money from the gamblers and from me to build the church and before it was finished they began to plan to run the sports out of town and close the saloons. I never knew any gambler to refuse to give man or woman help if they were in need; not like Carnagie, when the poor asked for bread he gave them a public library and answered this question:

"Dear readers: What class of people are benefited by these libraries?"

I had made arrangements to go into the mountains to look at some mining property and the railroad went up as far as Crister Butte, but all this trouble coming on I knew nothing about it. It seemed to change me, for I was determined to be rid of it all, so I had a talk with Mickey and told him he must vacate the place as soon as he could get one, for I would close his saloon up.

He said:

"If you will marry me I will never drink another drop of any intoxicating liquor, but will be a good man."

His mother prayed on her dying bed that he should be good and go back East and sell his property and go into his old business, a dry goods merchant.

I was to sell out as soon as I could.

He had always treated me with the greatest respect. If a man would say a vulgar word in my presence he would knock him down, for he was a fearless man and knew no fear.

I said:

"That leaf is not in my book. If you had millions I would not marry you, so never breathe a word about that subject again."

He said:

"You go to the mountains tomorrow morning and your wish is that I would be gone when you come back."

I said:

"Yes, that would suit me."

He said:

"No one regrets more than I the trouble I have foolishly brought upon you, but I did not think of getting you into trouble or I would never have brought him here, and although I am an outcast out here I was brought up to be a gentleman and have the education of one,and I have watched you closely at times when you never dreamed of such a thing, and for the first time in my life, I find a woman with two distinct characters, as though they belonged to two separate bodies. At times you are gentle and sympathetic and your look is far away as though not on earth, and at such times you are more like an angel than a woman of earth. Then you are changed, you know! you know no fear. I watched you when you shot the gun from Jim's hand and it did not excite you in the least, no more than if you had shot at a post—calm, cool and straighter home I never saw but with it all it was to save the other man's life, and when you came back you will find all my bills on the file; everything is paid for, and I will give you all there is before I go. I will not want anything."

I said:

"I hope you will never want barroom fixtures again."

He said:

"I have one favor to ask of you before we part, and that is, when I am gone you will pardon all the mistakes I have made and think kindly of me sometimes, and send a prayer to your God for pardon to one whose life has been all a mistake, and when I breathe my last breath on earth it will be, 'love for you, my fairy queen,' good-bye!"

He took my hand and kissed it, then he turned away and wept bitterly.

"I did not think you were a man of such strong feelings, and as for tears, I did not think you knew what they were."

I was surprised. I went to my room and to bed, but yet I was troubled, for there was something in his manner that I did not understand.

The next morning I got a light breakfast and started. It was very cloudy and the girl, Anna, said it was going to snow. "If I were you I would not go."

I started and before I got to the depot it began to snow, but I got my ticket and got on the car and as we started the wind blew a fearful storm. It came down in torrents. I tried to get a hack when I got there, but none were out, for the weather was too bad, so I went as best I could to the only hotel there was, "The Forest Queen," and there was a blazing fire in the fireplace and pitch was burning. That was a welcome sight to me. That night Sas, one of the owners of the coal mines, came, as they were boarding at the hotel, and said:

"Such a storm was never known."

The trains were all stopped. A train with twenty car loads of coal was blocked and as we were talking about the mines a telegram came for me to come home as fast as I could, as Jeff had taken poison. I could not get back, for it was impossible. As I was going to bed another telegram came saying that Mickey was dying. I went to bed, but not to sleep, for the wind blew fiercely and moaned and whistled. It was awful. Towards morning I fell asleep, but had not slept more than one hour when I was awakened by the landlady with a telegram saying that Jeff was dead.

This is what he meant that where he was going

he would not want any of his things. Poor boy! I felt sorry for him, but as soon as the storm stopped they put on the snow plows, and when the night passenger train left I was on it. When I got to Gunnison there was a crowd of men to meet me, and the mayor of the city had a carriage for me. We drove up to "Jack's Cabin." It was all dark but the No. 2 dining room, and I went in there. When I got in it was full of men. Jeff was a favorite among the boys, and be belonged to the G. A. R. and to the Odd Fellows. He went as a drummer boy in the rebellion.

They told me how they walked him up and down and slapped him with wet towels and boards, and how he begged for them to get me so he could see me when he closed his eyes forever, and he told all the boys he did not want to live without me, and for them to let him die. He wanted to go away forever. He had written two letters, one for his only sister and the other for me, and had told a friend where he had left them, but when I went to look for them there was only one and that was addressed to his sister. The one I should have gotten was missing. He told Anna that he had told me where I could find money in the letter, and he must have told John the same, for the man had money after Jeff was buried.

He had a very large funeral. He was buried in a fine black shroud and a $125 casket. I paid for everything, and after the funeral the saloon men got together and gave a bond and got Jim out of jail. He was all broken about Jeff. It was not long after that my trial came up and I was acquitted. Jim's trial came up and he was acquitted on the grounds of self defense. He left town and went to Montrose and got on the police force. He had not been on six months when he got into some trouble with cattle men and they formed an alliance and got him out of jail and his body was never found, and that was the end of him.

Both Jeff and I had a great many friends in Montrose and they blamed Jim for the death of Mickey and getting me into such trouble. That made them more severe on him, for one of the cattle men came to me and told me Jim had killed five different men, and they would see that he killed no more.

A short time after this trouble the two railroads were finished and hundreds of people had left Gunnison to go to the Ute reservations as soon as they were opened. Montrose, Grand Junction and Delta were all in Gunnison county, but they had divided and went by themselves and left all the debts to Gunnison to pay. They had not been gone long when Gunnison was deserted. They had built churches and the first to close was one in which the policeman got whipped and driven away. The Methodist was the only one for a long time. The lower town was a wreck.

I went into the mountains in Wild Cat Gulch where the Indians camped, and such a place for game! There was a small lake full of fish, and antelopes by the hundreds. Deer and all kinds of wild animals; prairie hens went in droves and elks would throw their large horns on their backs and turn their faces up to the sky and run through the timbers with the peculiar whistle that they had. And it would not be safe to get in their way while they are running.

I had four men with me, hunting for some rich gold ore, but we could not find where it came from, but we found a large vein of $20 to the ton, but it would not pay at that time to work it, so I let it stand. A prospector had brought me some silver ore that he got forty miles from Gunnison, but the claim was owned by three parties. I went to look at it and they had been digging in some black zinc. I went prowling around until I found some black stones, and in a crevice near those boulders I found some pure silver. I marked the place and said nothing, but found out the owners; one that owned a half interest had left and abandoned his interest. I wrote him and made him an offer. He sent the deed to the bank by return mail and so I became half owner of the Black Queen mine. There was no road to it then but the county commissioners had let the Rock Creek road to three of the South Park contractors, Dunbar, Shafer and Walsh, for $60,000. Walsh had been boarding with his nephew at my place for a long time, off and on, so he came and wanted to board the men when they were in town. He was a tall, fine-looking old gentleman, and was a warden of the Catholic church, and a widower. He had been very courteous to me at all times, but now he came right out and asked me to marry him. He had property in Cleveland and had plenty to take care of me. So I thought, well, I am nothing but a prey for everyone to plunder, that I have dealings with. Being alone, it seemed as though I was public property for everyone to rob, for the men I sent to the mine ate up the grub and drew their pay and did no work for it when I was not there. As this man was twenty years older than I, I would have a father as well as a husband, and so I said I would think of it, and two weeks later this Walsh came in from camp and said he had to go to Denver on business, and I had better go with him and we would get married, and without thinking I took my small satchel and not even a change of clothing, and took the train and went with him.

We went to the St. James Hotel and he got the license and made arrangements for Bishop Macerby to marry us the next morning.

That night I was awakened three different times by children crying, and yet it sounded as though they were a distance off. The next morning it worried me and I felt more like going to a funeral than a wedding and if I had had one friend that had said, "Don't marry that man," I would have backed out, for I felt that there was something wrong. I could not tell just what it was. After I was dressed I sat down in my room and waited for him to come. He did not come till near nine o'clock; then we went to breakfast, then to the Catholic Cathedral. He said he had to get permission from the Bishop to marry me, as I was not a Catholic, and that was what made him late.

He noticed the gloom that came over me and said:

"Cheer up."

I said:

"I don't know, but I feel I am doing wrong in getting married, and I would rather go to the depot and go back as we came."

He said:

"I did not think you were such a coward."

That touched me. I said:

"I am no coward, but I would not live with a man for whom I had no respect, even if I were married by every priest in the country."

When we got to the church there was a man and a woman, some friends of his, to stand for us, and I did not like them. A priest and a bishop came in and started the ceremony, and when the bishop said:

"Will you have this man for your lawful husband?"

The children set up such a crying and a man's voice said "No," so close to me that I jumped back and the ring fell to the floor and rolled to the priest. He stood by the bishop and stooped and picked it up and handed it to Walsh. He grabbed my hand and put the ring on my finger without any more ceremony. I thought all of them had heard the voice, it was so plain. It was as though a black pall had been thrown over me, for I knew nothing till I was in the vestry room and told to sign my name in a book. When we got outside he said to the man and woman:

"We will get a carriage and see the sights."

We went all around till about one o'clock, then went back to the hotel for dinner, and after dinner we bade good-bye to the couple.

Walsh said he had to go and see about some business and he left me. I sat in the room till about five o'clock; then he did not come, so I took my satchel, went to the depot and bought a ticket and left on the 6.20 train. I left word by the clerk to tell Walsh, if he came before the train left, to come to the train, for I was going to leave by it.

I got in Gunnison the next morning and I was glad to be home again and the gloom wore off. Then I thought what a bride I was. It was nearly two weeks before Walsh came home again and he was very affable. He stayed home only two days, then went to his camp, so I did not see much of him.

When the first of the month came it was pay day for the men. They all came to town to get their pay. They stayed in town two days, then went back to camp. Everything went on all right for a few months, when the road was finished, then Walsh came home and said they did not have enough money to pay the men, and that they could not get the warrants until the commissioners met and accepted the road, and they did not sit till the first of the month, and as it was only the fourteenth the men could not wait till the commissioners sat. I said nothing, but the next day Walsh came and said he had a talk with his partners and that they all agreed to give me $200 when they got the warrants if I would go on a note with them all for $2,600 to pay the men. It was only for such a short time that I would be nothing out. He said I had better make the $200. I said:

"I do not like to sign notes, and you had better get somebody else."

But he said to keep on, and said when there was a chance to make money I kicked it over. He said he would be there when the warrants were issued, and that he would take care of them. But still I had that same feeling as when I married him, and nothing had come of it, so I went to the bank, but when I got there the others were not there.

Walsh took a note from his pocket with his name on it and gave it to me to sign. I said:

"Why, this is your note; where do the others come in?"

He said he would take the note to the others to sign as soon as I signed it. I signed the note, but as soon as I had signed it the same voice said:

"Be silent and watch."

That night the men came in. They had all been to the office to get their pay and when they got back they were very angry and made threats, as they only got half of it and had to wait two weeks to get the balance, and as there was no work for them they had to leave. Most of them boarded with me and they went away and never paid their board. Some of them gave me orders to get the balance of the money. The next day nearly all of them had left town and I did not see much of Walsh, as they were busy settling up, and were under bonds to complete the road.

The 1st came and the commissioners sat, but no warrants came and Dunbar and Shafer had gone to Denver to look for another contract; that is what Walsh said.

I asked him why the note was not paid. He said he would look after that. The note was long past due and the cashier sent for me. He took me in his private office and said:

"You are a Mason's widow, and I am a brother and am sorry to have to tell you that several of us have been watching your affairs a little, and we find out that you have been duped by the man Walsh. He is not what he represents himself to be, and you will have to pay every cent of that note.

I said:

"What about the warrants?"

He said:

"They have signed for $60,000 but they only got $30,000. The other $30,000 went to the commissioners, $10,000 apiece for giving them the contract. They have lost at least $5,000, as there was more rock work than they thought. There is not one dollar coming to them, and the other two have skipped out, no one knows where, and Walsh would have gone too, but he is going to try to get your "Black Queen" mine, so be on the lookout, for we all think that he must have hypnotized you or you never would have married him after refusing such a handsome man as Mickey and one that worshipped the ground you walked on. Walsh tried to get your money from the bank, but we did not let him have any."

I said:

"How is it he had to pay all the money?"

The cashier said that he had overdrawn the warrants $1,600, and if he had not paid it they would have put him in jail for embezzlement, for the partners knew nothing of it until they came to a settlement. The other $1,000 he had sent away, so he had not gotten a cent of it. "You have $1,800 in the bank to your credit."

I said:

"Make out a check for it and put it on the note and I will pay the rest as soon as I can."

He said:

"We have sold out to the other bank, as there is not business enough for two banks in this town now, but it will be all right in the other bank, for you are good for it, but let me caution you; be on your lookout for that man, he would not hesitate to take your life to get that mine."

I had been saving up my money to get the winter supply for the mine, as the snow would be too deep to go in or out till May or June, so all that was wanted had to be put in before the snow fell. As I went out of that bank I could not describe my feelings, for I knew now that I had been robbed, and in the toils of a robber and a murderer, and I felt my lonely, almost God-forsaken condition. If the earth had opened and let me in, it would have been a blessing. When I got home there was a gang of men and it took my attention for a while.

CHAPTER VIII.

THREE days after this, I went in No. 1 building. It was deserted; only Walsh's nephew had the back room, near the backdoor, and as I got in the hall I heard angry words. When I got opposite the room No. 7, where Jimmy McClease used to sleep, a mysterious voice said:

"Come in and be silent."

I opened the door as quietly as I could and went in and did not quite close the door, but held it ajar so I could hear what was going on.

Johnny said:

"You promised me the money, and I want to get out of this place, for she asked me for my board money, and when I told her you would settle it she said that you had not paid your own board, and that she would not keep any man, and you mark my words that you will have to run against a sang, and if she gets onto your having a wife living she will put you through for what you have done."

Walsh said:

"I will take care that she does not get me for I will put her where she will not do any harm."

Jim said:

"Well, I want the money you promised me, and if you do not get it for me I will send to Leadville for my sister to come here and tell the Captain that she is your lawful wife for I am determined that you shall not dupe me with your damned lies, and I tell you to get the money, and quick, too, and we will see who will come out on top."

They went out of the back door and I flew out of the side door and up town before they got out of the front, and when I came back I had my hands full of bundles and went in the front door. Walsh was waiting at the door for me. He said a man had been to see him about getting a contract and there would be big money in it if he could go at once and see about it. I said:

"Well, why do you not go and look after it?"

He said:

"I have no money just now or I would go out on tonight's train. If you will let me have $50 I will pay you back when I get the county warrants."

I said:

"I have been to the bank and they have to have the note paid. I told them to attach the warrants, but they found out that there are no warrants; they have all been drawn. Now, I want to know who will pay the note?"

He looked as though a mask had been thrown off of his face, for instead of the smiling, religious, old gentleman, he looked like an incarnated demon, and such a hellish, fiendish look I never saw on a human face before. He turned away for a few minutes to calm his anger, then came to me and said:

"If you give me the fifty I will get the contract and pay every cent."

I said:

"I never will give you $50 or take your word for anything, and you will oblige me by getting out of my house, for you have misrepresented everything, and I refuse to live with you any longer."

He said:

"Half of this property is mine and half of all your mines are mine. I married half of everything you owned when I married your doll face and yellow head, and, by God, you shall not rob me out of my interest."

Then he began with a volley of curses, and the vilest language that tongue could utter, he used. I left that night. I slept with the girl. The next day was election day. The girl had gone up town and the house seemed empty, only there were two young men reading in the office-room. I sat reading a paper when Walsh came in with a paper and ordered me to sign it without reading it. I refused. Then he said:

"You will sign it."

And when I read it it was an agreement that I gave him half of all my property and half of all my mining property and all the mining property I would own for the next five years and when I had read it I opened the range door and threw it in the fire. He grabbed me and tried to stick my head in the fire. I clung to him and screamed until the two men came and took him by the collar, and then he let go of me. I ran to my room and got a gun and began to fire it outdoors, and then the officers came.

I said:

"I give this man in charge; take him out of my house."

They took him. He began to fight, but there were too many for him. My hair was nearly all burned and my face and neck were in blisters. I had to get the doctor to dress the burns. I sent all of his things out of my house to a friend of his and sent Johnny's things with them.

Then I sent word to them both that if they came to my house again I would shoot them down as burglars.

The next morning I went up with my attorney and showed my burned face. The court fined him $50 and costs. Then I swore out another warrant for him to keep him under bond to keep the peace, and they bound him over to keep the peace for three months and a $5,000 bond. He had a very valuable gold watch and chain and a gold-headed cane, so he gave them to his friend Macky for his fine, but had to stay in jail until he could get bond.

That night there was a tall, handsome, well-dressed young man came to see me. I did not recognize him at first till he said:

"You soon forget your old friends."

Then I said:

"Why, Hall, the cowboy! how you have changed, and it seems you always find me in trouble."

Then I told him all, and if I could only find out about where Walsh married his wife, so that I could get proof. I gave Hall the description of Johnny, so that he might try to see him and get what he could out of him. He went away and said that he would see me again. The next day Walsh got bond on condition that he would leave town. I said to the girl Anna:

"We must watch that Walsh, for he will do something before he leaves."

So when night came and he did not take the 6:00 train I got my gun and watched all I could, for I did not want to frighten the girl. She went to bed at 10:00 and at 11:00 I put out the lights as though I was going to bed, but sat and watched at the side windows, where I could see everyone who came down the street.

I was just going to my room when I heard a faint noise, and looking out through a crack in the door saw two men doing something under the window where my bed was. I ran as fast as I could to the side door and opened it quietly and took aim at the tall man, as I knew that he was Walsh, and the ball struck him in the leg. Then he let out a curse that he would kill me. I sent another bullet whizzing through his arm. The other man pulled him away and they boarded the freight train. They went through at 3:00 at daylight. The next morning I went to see what they were doing and found twelve sticks of giant powder with a coil of fuse and four caps, so they were going to blow up me and the buildings, too, had it not been for that other side of me, as Mickey called it, for I was determined I would have no more of his bulldozing or be in the same vibrations with such demons in the form of men. I had not been to bed and no one was up yet. I opened the barroom door and went in and stood on the very spot that I left Mickey weeping the last time, and such a feeling of loneliness and woe came over me that I stood as though rooted to the ground.

Only a few months ago I was as merry and cheerful as a meadow lark in spring, with a good bank account, and did not owe a cent. Now I was in debt and they kept sending in bills that Walsh had gotten, and began to sue me for the money that he had contracted in my name. Then self-remorse seemed to take possession of me and I groaned aloud:

"Oh! why did I marry him, and what is this power force?"

I was conscious that I was doing wrong and even the ring was dashed to the floor by unseen hands. It could not be spirit power, but a power far stronger than that which forces us to our destiny, and we ought to be on our guard all the time for strangers that we know not, for some people carry a straight light around them that is destruction to one that carries the opposite light. For when a murder wave or a suicide wave comes to a city you will know there will be many before it travels on, and those who fall by them are people that they surround, or are in harmony with the dark death wave, not those who are in the light.

There is a triangle of three powers that govern both heaven and earth—electricity, vibration, and this force power, I know not what to call it, but it comes in waves and in different colors and does its work according to its color. It is plain to see that Walsh attracted the dark, destructive way and came to a house of light and brought nothing but loss and misery, and would have murdered me if the same power only in the light was the strongest around me, so failed the dark. That is what saved me. This power is the strongest, as it pushed the electricity and pushed the vibration, and the almighty waves in the ocean are all curtailed by it. Nations rise and fall by it, and when the saints turn their attention to it we will have airships, and farmers will use it instead of horses, and all trains and cars will be pushed by it. Vibration is only known by wireless telegraphy. One little spark of it only, and there is no place on earth that will show this force as lively as in the mighty mountains. With the electric light sparks, with the vibration or echo of the roar of the wild animals in the dead of the night teaches a mind many lessons. I stood thinking of my troubles until I thought I should go mad, and I heard children singing hymns I used to sing when a child. When they stopped singing a child said:

"Fret not, mamma, but go away from this place, for we all love you so much, poor, dear mamma, good-by till we come again."

I stretched out my hands and cried out:

"Come back and take me with you."

Then I fell to the floor in a fit of weeping till I thought my heart would break. I must have been in this place for over two hours for Anna came to me and said:

"I was frightened to death, for when I went to call you to your breakfast I found out that you had not been in bed. I looked everywhere for you and you are in the very place where Mr.

Mickey nearly broke his heart over you. Come away."

She threw her arms around me and brought me to the dining room, but I was sick and had to go to bed. I was taken with a violent pain in my side and went into spasms. The doctor said I had a violent attack of gall stones, and I would cry out with the pain in my side.

Aunt Susan, a colored woman, who had been working for me ever since I was in town, came to take care of me, and the place was closed between my spells. I sent for S. Gill, the banker, and gave him all my jewelry and silver and papers of value, with the keys of my trunk, and told him what to do in case of death, as the spells were getting harder. I thought I would go crazy, as the pain was more than I could stand. They gave me morphine and chloroform, but I still had the pain, and the next day the doctors said that the stone was too large to pass and the only thing that would save me would be to call in a surgeon at once and have an operation. They were going to have a special train to bring Dr. Cochem from Salida, when Aunt Susan was crying as I lay across the bed.

A spasm came over me and I threw out my feet quickly and knocked Aunt Susan against the wall with such force that it nearly stunned her, and the violence of the sudden jerk unlodged the stone.

That night I had a congested chill that nearly took me. They had hot irons to my feet and worked with me for two hours; then I fell asleep and did not wake till next morning, but I did not get over it for several weeks.

When I began to sit up, Anna told me Hall had been to see me every day. He had to go away, but would come back, as he had something to tell me, and in ten days after I was up Hall came and told me he had gotten Johnny drunk and found out that Walsh was married to his sister by a justice of the peace and had two children, and that he was a Molly McGuire and a murderer in Pennsylvania, and that he had horsewhipped a priest on the altar for denouncing the Molly McGuires. Johnny was not with him when he tried to blow me up, but another man, a morphine fiend.

Walsh had promised him $5,000 from the "Black Queen" mine if he would help him get way with me, and he had not done with me yet, for he would sneak back and fix me, for he swore he would not be cheated out of my property.

Hall had gone to the mining camp called Aspen, and there was a big boom on, so I got him to get me a place to move some of my things to and start up in business there, so he went and in a few days I received a letter telling me of a good chance, but it had to be secured at once. He had paid $10 for one month's rent. I could not go, for I was too weak and sick. I got a man and Aunt Susan to pack everything we wanted to take, and the week after we started with three heavy loads, two with four and one with two horses. I went with the teams and it took us four days. We camped out three nights, and when we got to the place I found it was one of the best corners in the town. It was an old log cabin and I got carpenters and tore off the front and put in a store window and a new front; then it looked like a business place.

As soon as the boys knew I had come to town they all crowded the house and I had more than I could take care of. The old lady who owned the place got sick and sent for me and I paid her some money down and gave her a trust deed and bought the property. As I made money I built a rough board building, and I soon had $400 a month as rent coming in and was making money fast again, when that evil genius Walsh came. He was not under bond to keep the peace in that county and the third day that he was in town he began to sue me for half of all my property. I got a good lawyer and told him everything. He advised me to send for my pension, as Walsh was not my husband, but I had to set the marriage aside as absolutely void, so I brought suit against him for divorce. When the trial came he had five different men that I had never seen, to swear against me, one the morphine fiend. He was with him when he tried to blow me up, and two were penitentiary men, who had just got out and were broke, and he was going to make them rich if they would help him get the property from me, but it was no good; the jury said if I was what he tried to make me out he would not want to keep me, but would be trying to get rid of me. I won. The suit he brought had to be tried in Gunnison, as he had made another contract out and forged my signature and he tried to blacken my character. He told terrible things of me, and all false. He stole a very fine span of mules and wagon and harness out of my barn at night and got one of the witnesses to drive them away. I had to pay $500 for the outfit. I went to the sheriff, but he did not try to get them back, for Walsh had told him he had paid for them, and a lot of slander, so I had to go to Gunnison and get another lawyer to defend the suit. When it came to trial he had the fiend and the same witness that he had on the divorce case to swear they saw me sign the contract. My attorney had gotten the date of one of the prisoners, and he was in the pen at the time, and as soon as he found this out, he skipped out. The judge could see through the game and I won the suit.

Some of the men in town sent him a notice to leave town or they would attend to him, for they were sick of his game. They knew he was trying to rob me and would not stand for it, so he left. I sent in my pension papers as the attorney had advised me to, and waited for over a month, but they did not come. I received a latter from Gunnison that I would be arrested by the United States district attorney for trying to draw a pension when I had married. Walsh sent a copy of the marriage to the pension department in Washington, but did not tell that he was a married man at the time, so I had to get a Pinkerton detective to find out who married him to wife No. 1 and the witness to the marriage.

I had to neglect my business and it took all

the money I could get to defend all these suits, and the attorneys held me up, for they knew I had a good mine and they wanted to get a slice out of it. The attorney charged me $500 for the divorce suit, and the Denver attorneys, two of them, $1,000 apiece to defend the case in the United States Court before Judge Hallet.

Walsh was afraid of his wife, so he sent her to Canada, where they could not get her as a witness. I gave bond in Denver for $5,000 and did not leave until after the trial, and when the trial came Walsh was there as prosecuting witness, but when he saw the judge and the three witnesses to his marriage, he got out as fast as he could and went to Canada.

The judge told the jury that they could not find me guilty of perjury by signing my name Ellen E. Jack, for that was my name, and I had no right to any other. The jury was out about ten minutes and brought in a verdict of not guilty, and I was honorably discharged from the court. When I was discharged all the jury came and shook hands with me. The district attorney made out papers to have Walsh arrested for bigamy and perjury, but the bird had flown, and I learned that his wife and two children had all died of diphtheria in six weeks after they got into Canada. Walsh had gotten a contract on the Canadian Pacific and had made over $50,000 on it, and after that had gotten a contract on the Oregon Short Line and had made a large sum of money and was considered a wealthy man.

The morphine fiend was taken to a hospital

in Denver, where he told all that Walsh had promised, and as he was dying he cursed Walsh for his villiany.

I stayed in Denver two days after the trial, then went to Gunnison, then to the "Black Queen" mine, as I had leased it, but they were not to take any mineral out of the ground till the payment was made, and when I got there I was surprised to see all the sacks full of ore and ready for shipment, about three car loads. When I saw the foreman he told me he expected the jacks to take the mineral to the depot and ship it to the Denver smelter, and he said he guessed they did not reckon on my coming back so soon.

I said:

"Well, they will not take this mineral till they have complied with their contract."

At this time Mr. Aller came up to me and said:

"Why, we did not expect you here."

I said:

"By the looks of things I don't think you did, and I have had notice from the bank that there has been no payment on the bond, and until there is you cannot move that mineral."

He said in a sneering way:

"And who will stop me?"

I said:

"I will."

He laughed in my face. I went down the trail to the "Fargo cabin" and said to the three men that owned the "Fargo cabin:"

"Lend me your rifles and your shot gun; load them and give me some rounds of shot."

They did, and also helped me carry them to a bush on the "Queen" grounds.

I paid them to watch that night and stayed in their cabin, and another miner came from Crystal, the little town at the foot of the trail. He said that there were three jack punchers and a big herd of jacks, and they were coming to the "Queen" early in the morning to take the mineral. I went to the "Queen." When I heard the dogs barking and the bells ringing on the jack's necks, as they always have trained dogs and have bells with a herd of pack donkeys, I got one of the men to help me carry the rifles down to the dump, where all the sacks were filled up, and put the rifles by them. I had my two .44's with me and I stood by the sacks. As the bark of the dogs came nearer, Mr. Aller came to the dump and when he saw me he turned as white as death and said:

"What in hell are you doing here?"

I said:

"I am on my own ground and you are a thief, and I have the right to protect my property. Your bond and lease are forfeited. You get off this property."

By this time the jacks were coming on the jump. I stopped them. Then the owner came to see what was the matter.

I said:

"Mr. Benton, turn your jacks off this property, for not one sack of mineral leaves this place."

Aller had jumped upon the shaft house and got his check book out and was swinging it around and yelling:

"A thousand dollars if you take that mineral."

Then Benton blew his whistle as a signal for his two men to crowd the jacks, and as the leaders pushed upon the dump I shot them down. Benton tried to get his big gun out of his belt, then I sent a shot and took his ear off as clean as though it had been cut off, and was going to send another, when he threw up his hands and yelled out:

"I am shot."

I sent a shot and shot the check book and two of the tips of Aller's fingers off; then he began to yell. I changed the gun from the left hand to the right, then Aller jumped off of the shaft house and got behind some logs. I said to Benton:

"Turn your jacks and go down the trail."

He said:

"You will shoot me when I pass you."

I said:

"I do not want your miserable life and if you do as I tell you I will not hurt you."

Then he came and he was bleeding awfully.

I said:

"Wet your handkerchief and put it to your head and stop the flow of blood."

He blew his whistle and had the jacks turn and went to his pony and got to town as fast as he could to get his wounds dressed. Aller had sneaked out and down the trail to get the morning train to Gunnison to get me arrested. When I looked around there was not a man, for they had all gone to the mine to escape the shots. I was all alone and I could not describe the contempt, that I had for these cowards. There I was with three bad men armed with big Colt .44's and Aller with his check and 32 men left me all alone to defend myself and property. When all was over they came up like whipped curs, but I turned and went down the trail.

All was excitement in the camp. I went to the Fargo cabin and sent one of the men for the rifles. I knew they would not be wanted again, so I waited for the sheriff to come. One of the men had gone to Crystal to find out what he could, and he heard the jack man say that I had killed seven jacks. They rolled down the hill two thousand feet into Broth creek, so if I had not killed them the fall would have. The jack men were making big threats. Benton had gone to the mountains to get a doctor.

The next day the sheriff came with a warrant for me. He had bought the finest span of horses and rig that he could find in Crystal. That was as far as they could go, and when we got through to Crested butte we had to stay till the train went to Gunnison the next morning.

The sheriff had engaged the best room in the best hotel in town for me. There was a show in town that night and I said:

"Doc." (that was the name the sheriff went by), "what are you going to do with me? I want to go to the show."

He said:

"Go where you like, only be on time for the train in the morning."

I said:

"Tell them to get me up, for I have had no sleep for two nights and will be sleepy in the morning."

So I went to the Fealen House and told Mrs. Fealen to come with me to the show. We were a little late, so when we were going down the street there was an excitement and the miners shouted:

"Hurrah for our mountain queen!"

I stood and faced the crowd; then they clapped their hands and shouted:

"Brave woman! our mountain queen!"

Then I bowed to them and sat down. As soon as it was known what I had done there was quite an excitement. It seemed that every one but myself was excited, for they expected to see me a prisoner, and there I was with a woman at the show.

After the show the miners waited for me to come out; then they shook my hands nearly off and I was afraid they would pick me up and carry me on their shoulders to the hotel. I had to beg them not to, for they shouted:

"Let's carry her."

Crested butte is a coal-mining town and the end of the railway, and there are quite a number of English whom they call "Cousin Jacks," and they are very fond of anything that is gritty, or as they call it, plucky, and the report was that I had killed some men. I knew nothing of that till afterwards. There were all sorts of stories going about. I was glad to get away and go to the hotel, and the next morning before daylight they were pounding on my door for me to get up.

I went and got a cup of coffee and went to the depot to wait for the train, and nearly every one that came to the depot came up to me and shook hands. As soon as I got on the train I went to sleep, and when we got to Gunnison there was quite a crowd to meet us. A carriage was waiting and Aunt Susan pushed her way thorugh to me and threw her arms around me and said:

"The Lord bless you, I have cried a wash tub full of tears. How many did you kill?"

I said:

"I do not know, but they say I killed seven."

She said:

"Oh, the good Lord, they will hang you seven times."

And she began crying again. I thought the people had all gone crazy. There was so much excitement. The sheriff came to me and said:

"Get in the carriage and go home and I shall send for you when I want you."

Then he said to Aunt Susan:

"Have you got the captain's breakfast ready?"

She said:

"No, they said you were going to lock her up."

He said:

"Get in with her."

Then he told the driver to go to "Jack's Cabin" and leave me there, and as the carriage started the crowd set up a shout and we dashed out and were soon at my home.

Aunt Susan jumped out and opened the door. She had a good fire, for it was very cold, and she got me a light breakfast. Then I told her I was going to lie down and for her not to let anyone bother me. I picked up my guitar and played and sang "Home Again from a Barren Shore."

"Fo 'de good Lord, you would play and sing if you saw the rope on de gallows waiting to hang you after you had killed seven men; you sing as though nothing had happened."

I said:

"Who said I killed seven men?"

She said:

"Why, you told me yourself that you killed seven."

I said:

"I did not say seven men, I thought you meant the jacks I killed."

She said:

"They say you killed a lot of men, and that is why there is so much excitement."

So I began to see why the men seemed to be crazy. I went to bed and to sleep, for I was worn out. I little bit before 10 o'clock the deputy came and told me to be at Judge Piper's court at 10 o'clock, so I dressed and went up to the court. My attorney was there with a copy of the bond and lease, and the courtroom would not hold half of the people who had gathered there to hear the trial. It was proven that if he had taken the mineral they would have put the money in their pockets and the mine would have to pay the men and all the debts that had been contracted against the mine, and if I had killed them I would have been justified, for if they had any right to the mineral they should have taken it by leave, not by force.

They had to pay all the costs, over $200, and as Aller was not a resident of that county they locked him up till he paid, for they thought he would skip out and not pay, as he would have done with me if he could have gotten the mineral.

Then the jack man wanted pay for his jacks, but I had ordered him to take them off of my property, and it was proven that he pulled his gun to shoot before I shot at him, so they all got the worst of it. I had my attorney notify Aller not to go on the "Queen" property any more, as his bond was forfeited. I was going back to work the mine myself. Then the sneery look on his face turned to one of hatred, for he knew he could not go back with me there, for the next time I took aim at him he would never come to have me arrested again. I went to Crested butte the next day and from there to the Queen with a small train of burros with provisions, for I had found out that there was not much of anything at the mine. The powder was all gone and nothing had been paid, for that had gone up to the mine. I began to get things straightened out before the snow came, as it was getting near winter, so I sent the jacks back packed with mineral and came and took it all. They sent it to Denver, and in four days returned with a check for it. Then I went and got it cashed and paid all the men and let two-thirds of them go, for I could not get powder and grub enough to keep them all winter.

Aller had a large force of men to get all of

Captain Jack Starting for Her Mines.

the ore out and skip out with it, so I kept a few of the best. I had to go to the mountains again and it took me three days to do the business I had to do; the fourth day I went back. It was late when I got to Crystal, and Crystal is a little over a mile below the "Black Queen" mine, at the foot of the trail. We began to climb at Crystal up to the mine. It was moonlight and I had ten pounds of beefsteak in a sack to keep the men going until the jacks came up two days later on, and when I had gotten to a place about half way up the mountain, where three trails come together, I stood rooted to the ground, for "crack!" went the bushes and two eyes like two balls of fire were close to me, for I did not see it till I was right on it.

I stood still, I dropped the beef and stood still for a few minutes, frightened nearly to death, for I had no gun and I did not know what it was. It was a large animal. It looked at me and I at it; then I got over my fright and put out my hand and said:

"You go your way and I will go mine. I do not want to hurt you nor you me, so go."

And as if it understood me it started down the lower trail. I waited to give it time, then I picked up my sack and started on the middle trail, and when I had gone about fifty yards the thing stopped and turned around to see if I were after it. I shouted:

"Go on; I want no truck with you. I like you best at a distance."

It smelled meat and did not know if I was the meat or not. I was getting very tired when the Fargo cabin came in sight. Then I began to whoop and two of the men came and carried my bag. I told them what I had seen and when I told them I trembled with fear. They laughed until the mountains echoed with the loud laugh at the very idea of my being afraid of a devil, let alone a mountain lion, for that was what it was.

We had another carload of mineral ready to ship and the jacks were bringing provisions up and taking loads of mineral back to the depot. It began to snow and we wanted to get all the provisions in before it got to be too deep with snow. At twelve o'clock at night it blew up a fearful storm and I went up and dressed, for the log cabin was in danger of a slide, and I was afraid that if the two trees above the cabin blew down they would take the cabin to the bottom of the river, which was over two thousand feet to the bottom of the mountain, and so steep that we could hardly stand when off the trail.

I heard big rocks rolling down the mountains and the winds whistled. The barking of the coyotes and the roaring of the bears were a fright. I would have gone to the mine and down in it, but I was afraid of rocks striking me. The mine was about seven hundred feet from the cabin and we had to pass a draw before we got to the shaft house, and all the slides came down that way. It was blowing and snowing fearfully. It started just as the graveyard shift shots went off and kept up for two days and nights, and we were in a fix, for we were not prepared for such a storm as this, and it was impossible for the jacks to come now, so we had to go on short allowance. I gave the men bacon for breakfast, steak for dinner and ham for supper.

The fourth day I said to the foreman:

"There is a pair of snow shoes; if they were fixed up I would try and get out on them."

So the men got them. They were eight feet long and they fixed them up, and got the pole fixed with a new spike at the end, and at five in the morning I started with the little dog Fan on my back, in a flour sack. I had to have shoes for the mountains were so steep and the brakes on the trail were covered with snow. I got down to Crystal and went in the only store there, and rested a short time. The man said I could not get to Gothic, for the snow was very deep in the Scafield Park.

All the miners had to leave several days before to keep from being snowed in, and the snow slides were coming down the mountain. He begged me not to try to go, but I could not go back to the "Queen" and I could not stop there, as it might snow, so I started. When I got to the park I looked for the log cabins, but could not see them. I saw one little black spout on the side of this mountain, so I sailed up to it and it was the top of a stovepipe. The cabins were all snowed under.

The sun was getting very high, when my face began to burn and I could hear the slides coming down the mountains like peals of thunder. When I got to the top of one mountain I had to pass what they called the "Windy Point." I prayed for a guide to take me past it safe, for it was the worst place on the road, and slide after slide came down and carried everything with them.

As I started to go quickly, Fan, the dog, began to whine. She must have scented danger, for she had never moved all the way until I got to this place. I stayed for a minute or two to get my breath before I shot around the point. As I stood a peal of thunder came, and down came a slide. As soon as it had gotten a safe distance I went like the wind so as to get over before another slide came, and I was not any too soon, as I could hear them coming in all directions. The hot sun loosened them and down they came. I would slide up to a tree once in a while and stand up against it and rest. Being on those long snow shoes so long gave me a backache. It was late in the afternoon and I had to go at least ten miles farther. It was quite dark when I got to Garyese's Hotel in Gothic, and when I took my shoes off some of the miners came to help me and when I went in the sitting room the boys said:

"Oh! you have got an awfully blistered face."

I said:

"I can hardly see; I believe I am going snow-blind, for I forgot to put black over my eyes."

One of the men took out his knife and stuck it in the big blister on my face and let the water run out and another got a raw potato and scraped it to put on my eyes to keep me from going blind, and the hot, burning feeling and my burning eyes and face and the dizzy feeling I had! I was in a pitiful plight. I could hardly go upstairs to bed and had to get the landlady to help me get in bed, and when I did I could not sleep till nearly morning. I did not get up until late the next morning, and then it was nearly noon, and I went and made arrangements to get a horse and go over the mountain pass to Aspen. They were at work cutting a road over the pass. The snow was not deep on the pass and the men were shoveling it where it had slid down.

So, early in the morning, there were five of us going on horseback over the pass, and it had snowed a little in the night. The next morning we all started. Two of the men were Hebrews, commercial travelers; the other two were merchants. We had not been on our way more than one hour before it began to blow and snow so thick that we could not see a yard before us. They all halted and said it was not safe to go on. They wanted me to turn back with them, for they would not go any farther, but I only laughed at them and waved my handkerchief adieu to them and went on alone. I had gone some distance and the snow was getting deep, when the horse had great difficulty in going through, and as I got to a point near the summit some of the men were bucking snow, trying to keep the road open, so that they could get provisions, as the men who were making the road were camped on the top of the Monroe Pass. There were 210 men and 60 mules, and the big draft horses with scrape plows and all kinds of tools to work with, and had it not been for the men on the road I never could have gotten up the mountains. I got around the point, and as it had slacked up a little I could see the tents and cabins. They looked like a little town, and as I got nearer some of the men came out to see who was coming over such a day, and when they saw a woman alone they ran in the tents and got all the men to come out and see the "mountain queen" brave the storm; and such a cheer! it echoed through the mountains. They took me out of my saddle and put the horse in the stable to feed him, and I went to the dining room, such as they had. I got some hot coffee and a lunch. I told them I would go, as they were making preparations for me to stay all night. They told me there was a wash-out on the trail, and a man tried to get over it and both he and his horse were killed. They both lay dead at the foot of the mountains, as the storm was too dangerous and severe for them to try to get them up; but as they were telling me, that mysterious voice kept saying, "Go on, go on."

So I said:

"I will go on and if I find that I cannot make it I will come back, as it is only two miles from here, and the horse is now rested and I want to make Aspen before dark, and it is getting late."

I got up and told the men to get the horse. They all looked at one another in a woe-begone way, for they thought I was doomed to death. I got in my saddle, then about six or eight men said they would go as far as the washout with me and see the end of me. I walked my horse, which took more time, and when the horse got to the place he stopped. I had to back him away from it, for the trail was narrow and so steep and the break was about three feet, but there seemed no footing on the other side. The voice was so stern, "Go on, go on." I went back some distance, then braced myself for the leap, and then I came on a run and a jump and over we went, but the horse trembled so after we were on the other side that I had to pat him and talk to him.

The shouts of the men were something terrible. I never turned my head to look at them, but the first time I got up to the place I saw the man and the horse dead at the foot of the mountain. I did not look again, but I could hear the shouts of the men for their "mountain queen," and as they went down the pass I could hear faintly their cheers. It was getting dark and I was on a very steep place, for the dog began to whine. I had not gone far before I met a big herd of jacks who blocked the trail, for I could not get past them. I dare not attempt to take the horse off the trail, and I tried to crowd them until I had lost all hope of getting them turned. I had already lost over one hour and it was getting very dark and cold, when all at once there was a roar of bears and the jacks got scent of them, and they all turned around as if by magic and I ran as fast as I dare, for the trail was slippery after the snow, and it was quite dark and late when I got to the foot of the mountain and came to where there were sleigh tracks. To the right there was a fence and to the left the tracks went to some timber. I had never been over this road before, so did not know which was the way, and it was too dark to see a yard before me. I thought the fence was a ranch, so took the left road and kept on going till I came to an old log cabin with no doors or windows and the chinking all out, but the horse could go no farther, and the whining of Fanny was pitiful, so I jumped off the horse and went in and took the horse in too, and there was a soap box that had been a feed box, so I broke it on the end of the logs and built a fire in the middle of the cabin; then I took the saddle off the horse, but had no supper for him. By the blaze of the fire I could see that something was wrong with Fanny, and when I examined her I found that her legs and feet were frozen as stiff as a bar of iron. I took my gun out to shoot her, and she knew what I was going to do, for she began to whine and the tears came down her cheeks as though she was human. Then I thought of what the boys had said to put snow on a frozen limb and it would draw out the frost. I put my gun back and took my knife and cut some of my underclothes into strings and bandages, then got some snow and bound it around her legs and feet. I had put some red pepper in my shoes before starting, so as to keep my feet warm, and that saved my feet from freezing. The horse lay down; he seemed to know there was something wrong, and there was no supper for him. I jumped around to keep awake, for I

Mrs. Captain Jack—Queen of the Rockies.

would have frozen to death if I went to sleep. I began to try to get some wood to keep the fire going. I looked at my watch and it was near three o'clock in the morning, when such shrieks, as though the Indians were tearing women to pieces, and cry after cry was something terrible; in the timbers and lost, not knowing how far I was away from any human being. The dog whined in fear and the horse pricked up his ears to listen and look at me. I spoke to him and kept the fire going, but such a night! Then the wind began to blow and the noise of the pines and the whistling of the wind and the terrible crying of something, I know not what; no pen can describe the feeling of loneliness and desolation, and animal and man seemed to come nearer to each other, for both horse and dog seemed to share my feelings, for they both looked as though they had pity to see me afraid. They gained courage from my looks, though not a word was said, and that is more convincing of the power of vibration from me. It was evident that I kept the gun in my hand, for I knew not what might come, but I made up my mind I would keep one bullet for myself, for I would not be tortured to death, for I would put the last bullet through my own brains before I would be abused. It seemed as though every minute was an hour, for I thought daylight would never come. and the later it got the colder it seemed to get.

I thought of the voice telling me to go on. It had deceived me for the first time, I thought, for if I had stayed with the boys I would have had daylight the rest of my journey and not put in such a dreadful night as I was having, and no one can imagine the thoughts that flew through my mind in the dead of night and in the hour of loneliness, in a forest with snow deep in the timbers and the screeching of something, I know not what. The sighing of the winds seemed to be chanting the requiem of some lost spirits, for nothing either on this earth or below the earth could be more dismal; as I stood, the fire died out, as I did not know where to get more wood to keep it going, and it seemed as though it was getting daylight, and as soon as it got a little lighter I put the saddle on the horse and put the bridle over my arm and took Fan in the other arm in my shawl and started to follow the sleigh tracks; they must take me somewhere and I walked for over two hours.

Then I saw an old sawmill, and when I got nearer I began to yell an Indian whoop, and four or five men came to the bunk house in their night drawers and called out:

"Is that Captain Jack? for no other woman would be out in this place on such a night but she."

I called out:

"You are right. It is I and I am nearly frozen and do not know where I am now. I started on my way to Aspen, but was delayed and could not see through the way, and of all the hellish screams and yells I heard I cannot tell."

The men said:

"Yes, that is the proper name for them. There are some dead cattle about two miles from here and the bears and panthers and coyotes and mountain lions are all having a scrap over them, and we have not got enough ammunition to go after them, but it is awful. Their snarls and cries in the dead of the night is enough to wake the dead."

I was in the cook house and a fire was getting both me and the room warm and the horse was getting fed, but poor Fannie's feet were as large as eggs. They were terribly swollen.

As soon as I got warmed up I started for Aspen. The road by the fence was the road I should have taken. I started out for another cold ride, but I had been going up hill all night and I would go down hill back, and as I went I could see plainly how I had gotten lost, and when I got to town I rode up to my place that a German had rented and told him to take the horse to the stable and I would go to another house and go to bed. I went and told my friends all about the night I had, and when I tried to get my boots off I could not. move them, and Mrs. B. had to come and cut them off and help me to undress, for I seemed to get numbed and my head whirled around, and it seemed I had not been in bed but a short time when Mrs. B. came and said:

"Captain, are you awake?"

I said:

"Oh! don't bother me. Let me sleep."

She said:

"The house is crowded with people and they are frantic with grief. What time did you leave the summit on Moraine Pass?"

I said:

"About four o'clock."

She said:

"And were all the men well and happy then?"

I said:

"They all seemed to be."

She said:

"You must come downstairs and see these people, for you were the last that saw them."

"Well, and what have I to do with them?"

She said:

"Why, do you know what happened last night?"

I said:

"Yes, I heard the most horrible groans and shrieks and cries. I hope I never will hear them again."

"Oh! Oh! then you must have heard them. Do not tell the poor people what you have heard, for it would set them crazy."

I said:

"Well, I did not go crazy, and I do not see why they should."

She looked at me so queer and said:

"Why, you did not lose your loved ones and they did."

I said:

"What do you mean?"

She said:

"Everyone of those men got killed last night, and all the horses and mules, and there is not one to tell the story. You were the last human being that spoke to them and saw them alive, and how you got here alive is a mystery."

Then I knew why the voice said, "Go on, go on."

A snow slide came down and took cabins, men and everything in its way; trees that had stood over one hundred years were swept away as though they had been straws, and as I thought, yes, the wind and the sighs of the pines were surely chanting the requiem of the dead.

She said:

"You must see these poor people. I cannot get dinner or do anything for the crowds that come to see you. Everything is excitement and gloom is on every face. The snowslide did not leave a man to tell the tale."

I went into the room. It was crowded mostly with women with swollen eyes from weeping, and as soon as they saw me they cried out:

"What did my Pat say? Did he send me a message?" and all kinds of such questions.

Well, I knew all the men by sight, but could not tell Pat from Bill, and there were over three hundred, with the teamsters, and sixty head of mules and large horses, and a snow-slide had come down and taken cabin, tents and trees that had stood for over one hundred years, and had left the side of the mountain as barren as though it had been cleaned with a scraper, and such distress! They seemed to cling to me for a message from their loved ones, and when I told them all were well and happy when I left them, some of them asked me why I did not stay. Then I thought of the voice and how ungrateful I had been, for I had made light of it in the night and said that it had misled me. Now I could understand why it was so determined for me to leave and kept on saying: "Go on, go on." I surely would have stayed and perished with the rest only for the voice, but I said nothing to the people, only that I had to get to Aspen as quickly as I could. So I started on. One poor woman said:

"There must have been some good spirit that took you away from that accursed place, and I wish the Lord had been as kind to my poor boys as he was to you, for I have lost all the support I had, my husband and two boys. I am afflicted and cannot work. Oh! what shall become of me? Oh! that I had perished with my blessed boys!"

She broke down and wept bitterly and every way I looked I saw nothing but tears and deep-felt misery. I could hardly stand it so I had to leave them and get to my bed again, thankful to the Creator, for this was worse than I thought, and I was sick in body and soul. I lay tossing for a time, then nature gave away and I slept sound till the next morning, and about noon the news came that a rescuing party of twenty had gone to see what they could do, and everyone of them had been lost. The mayor of the town gave orders for no one to go near the place.

The winter was a very severe one and it was a sight to see the little donkeys with 300 pounds of ore on their backs; three sacks, with 100 pounds in each sack, one on each side and one on the top of the pack saddles. They climbed on such a narrow path and the mountains covered with snow. The jacks had bells on their necks, and the tinkling of the bells and the barking of dogs and cursing of the jack punchers behind a trail of jacks keeps a camp pretty lively. Then the yells of the gamblers and music in the saloon and dance halls and in the mining camps where there are every class of people, and all on the alert to grab what they can.

I had got one of my houses back and had gone "batching." One day I went out and left my door open and when I came back there was a large mountain lion lying on my bed as contented as if it were at home. Now I did not like such a bedfellow, so I went to the corner and asked some of the men to get him. They said the marshal and a lot of men were looking for him. He had broken his chain and gotten away from a man who lived up town, but none of the men would go near him till the owner came. He went up to him and took him up off the bed, but the lion did not want to go. The man, Bob, said:

"Cap, did you ever have a scrap with one of these fellows?"

I said:

"No."

He said:

"Come here, I will show you something," and he got the lion's tail, and at the very end of it there was a sharp claw bowed like a fish-hook and covered with hair, all but a very little of the sharp point. When in a fight they swing their tails and tear whatever they happen to strike, and this makes them one of the most dreaded beasts in the mountains.

He put a new chain on him and took him away, but three days after he was shot by the order of the law. Some two weeks after this I was sitting by my open window when a pack of jacks came by, going to corral for the night, and as they passed the stench was fearful, and I noticed some of them could hardly walk. The jack punchers were yelling to the dogs to hurry them up. I do not know what struck me, for I sprang out of my door and after the jacks. I stood outside of the board fence watching them take their pack saddles off of the poor animals, and such a stench and such a sight I cannot describe, for there was not one whose back was not as raw as beefsteak. Two of the punchers got a piece of flat stick and scraped the maggots out of their wounds, and if the jacks moved they kicked them and beat them unmercifully. There were people who knew about this, but were afraid of the punchers, as they were a very bad set of men.

I went in search of a humane officer and got two who were just made officers, and the next morning I swore out a warrant for them and the officers got them, as they had all the saddles on over their poor wounded backs ready for another load to grind in a little deeper, and when they were arrested they swore that they would have revenge upon the one who dared to interfere with their business. None of the officers had been idle, for they had gotten a lot of witnesses, and I was late when I went in the court room, but when I was called I said:

"I swore out the warrant and what I had seen was enough to convict."

Then the judge fined them $50 and costs and ordered them to turn the jacks out to pasture and tend to them, and said if they worked any one of the wounded jacks he would send them to jail. The next day a man came to me and said:

"Captain, look out for yourself, as the punchers are going to do you up, and there are a lot of them on the corner. I jumped up and took my gun and went up to where there was a gang of punchers and tin-horn gamblers cursing, and I went in front of the man who had been fined and I said:

"You wanted to see me. I am here. Pull your gun, you cur," and at the same time I shot his hat off of his head. Such a scattering! Some men ran one way and some the other, and the man ran to the hospital, for he thought he was shot, but I only shot his hat off his head. That was all that they wanted of me, for I heard no more threats and knew that they would not dare to try to harm me, for they were a set of cowards to be such brutes to the poor animals that were making a living for them.

The spring had come on and I got word to go to Gunnison, as some one wanted to buy the "Queen," and as there was no railway I had to get a wagon and a man to drive, as we had to be on the road three nights and I had to wait till I could get a team and a man that I could trust. I found one after waiting ten days, so we started at dayreak to go by the way of Ashcraft and Tailor Park, and such scenery was beyond description. I could get one hand full of the most beautiful flowers and the other full of snow. Every color of flowers, the May finks blooming under the snow and the clear streams of water; and the Taiolr river with its speckled trout. The man could take a dishpan full in one hour, and the game was plenty. Deer and antelope in droves. It was a beautiful sight and on Saturday morning we got in Gunnison and on Monday I began to dicker for the sale of the "Queen," and that week closed a deal for $25,000, $5,000 down and the balance in one year. I paid up all that I owed and went out prospecting again, but found nothing but hardships and loss of money, and while I was waiting for the balance of the money the lawyers were busy how to get hold of it. They trumped up all kinds of things and charged me the most outrageous prices. The attorney who got my divorce charged $500 and another trumped up a case was $1,500. Amongst them they had $5,000 attorney fees. Such robbery I never thought would be tolerated, for there was not $100 due them; $50 was the price of a divorce, and $50 more would have paid them well for all that had been done, with what I had already paid, so they tied up $5,000 of my money and I had to pay it before I could give a clear title to the company. I was so disgusted that I left the place and went to Ouray, a prosperous mining town built on the side of the mountain, a very picturesque place, with hot water running through its streets in the winter. I found a good showing of silver up Bear Creek Falls, so went to work and built cabins and blacksmith shops and went shipping. It paid expenses whilst silver was up. I tried to sell and got a company that was to pay me $60,000 for the mine in ten days, as their president was coming from New York with the money and they were going to stock it for $3,000,000, and float the stock, and in five days after the contract had been made and the deed in the bank, silver went down and kept going down, and when the partner came with the money they decided to wait till silver went up, and are still waiting, for silver was denominated, and that settled it, so I lost a lot of money in that, and I was not the only one, for numbers of mines were closed down and men thrown out of work, and at this time a gold camp had started at Cripple Creek, and everyone that could get away, got; everyone wanted to sell and no one to buy. Houses were nailed up and the town seemed deserted. It was a sorry sight from the busy place it had been.

Some of my neighbors who went to Cripple Creek wanted me to go with them. I still had a lot of property in Gunnison, so I went back to look after it, as Gunnison was picking up a little. The ranches were all doing well and they were sending their children to school in the town, so I fixed up my houses and rented them, but there was nothing for me to do but watch my property, and that was too tame for me, so I decided to go West. My foreman and a ranchman that I had a note against and a neighbor widow woman with three boys got two big covered wagons and six fine horses and a big camping outfit, and Luey rented his ranch and we started for the wild West.

CHAPTER IX.

WE went through Utah, away around St. George, and on Christmas eve. we got in a Mormon town and camped at a farmhouse. The owner was an Indian with two wives, as pretty white women as could be found in New York. He had a large house and an organ, but no one could play on it. He invited us in. He gave us cake and wine and I got some of my music and played and sang for them, and they were delighted and wanted us to stay and go to church the next morning and sing at church, but we had too much expense. Feeding the horses cost a lot of money, camping every night in corrals, for we had to do that to get water and feed for the horses. The next morning when the men were going to get ready to start the Indian offered them $500 in gold to leave me, for he said he wanted me for his third wife and he must have me.

The men were afraid we would be stopped, as we were in the midst of Mormons, no one for miles but Mormons. They told him that he could not get me, for I was the property of the U. S. government, and that the government would send soldiers to get me. I knew nothing of this and all that was going on with the men.

I went to the house to get some butter, when the tall, handsome woman said to me:

"So you are coming over to us. He is going to marry you."

I said:

"You must be crazy, for I would not marry any man, let alone a man with two wives. Have no fear of me."

Then they both came to me and kissed me and said:

"Are you going away today?"

I said:

"As soon as the horses are hitched to the wagons."

So they gave me a crock of butter and a lot of nuts and cookies and I went to put them in the wagon. The Indian came to me and said:

"Stay with me. I will give you half of what I have, for I love you. I thought I loved my wives, but never felt for them as I do for you. I would be your slave willingly and you would be my queen. Have pity on me, Oh! fair woman, and stay and sing with that sweet voice of yours, for if you go I will pine away and my last thought will be of you. Oh! my love, my love."

He burst out weeping and sat on the tongue of a wagon. My men were hurrying as fast as they could and were almost ready to go away.

It was a beautiful, balmy Christmas morning and everything seemed in harmony but the poor man in tears. All were ready and I went up to him and laid my hand on his shoulder and said:

"Good-by; you will soon forget me. Be good to your wives, by-by."

Then I turned and got in the wagon and crack went the whip and off went the horses, and everyone of us were glad to turn our backs on that romantic and sleepy-looking little town.

We went two days on a sandy sea, and as we had narrow tires on and no barrels for water, it was awful. The third day we came to the Verden river. The horses drank so much that we lost two of the best ones, as the water was alkali and contained quicksand. We had to get over the river as quickly as we could or everything would go under the bottom of the river. Some left one wagon, then went and got it, and we made only five miles in some days. All the wagons out in that country are wide and have good wide tires and two big barrels of water, one on each side. We were not prepared for such a country and such a trip. The horses suffered for water. We bought water at ten cents a bucket from section houses on the railroads which run through the deserts. When we got near one they had tanks of water that the train brought and filled. It was warm and nasty but we were glad to get it when we could. We went on till we came to another Mormon settlement and stopped to get meat and supplies. There was a very pretty dark-eyed woman with three little children. She was chopping wood for the fire for dinner. I asked her if she had some beef for sale. She said that her husband would be in soon and he sold the meat. She asked me in to wait for dinner. When I went in there was another very pretty girl, seventeen years old, nursing a young baby. When the dark woman went out I asked her:

"How old is your baby?"

She said:

"It is not my baby. It is the other wife's

baby. I have only been married one week and the baby is five weeks old."

I said:

"Did you marry that woman's husband?"

She said:

"Yes, he is my husband, too. The other did not like it, but she could not help herself."

There was a large fire place in the room and a bright fire burning. I looked at the fire and thought of these poor slaves.

The woman with four children, one only five weeks old, and she could not have been over thirty years old, and had to chop wood, and then the washing and cooking to do for so many, for the yard was full of clothes that she had washed, and when the man came he had two other men with him, his hired men. I bought a yearling beef of him and some other things. He was a fair-haired Swede, about thirty-five years old.

He asked me to dinner and I went in and there he sat at the end of the table, a dark wife on his right-hand side and the fair girl at his left. A large piece of roast beef in front of him, fit for a king, with every kind of vegetable, and he had all the airs of a millionaire. I could not help thinking of the poor woman who had to cut the wood to cook all that nice dinner, besides doing the big washings, and a baby only five weeks old. Then for him to bring another wife to sit all dressed up with blue beads around her neck and bracelets on, doing nothing but holding the baby, so this is God's will and religion and Bible teaching!

After dinner I went to my wagon and told the men we would go on till we could find a place to camp, and at five o'clock we came to a good place to camp, and when the second wagon came up all were in a commotion. The three boys were swollen up like three poisoned pups and roaring with misery. Talk of Peck's Bad Boy, he was not in it. I knew they had been in some mischief, and when I came to find out what it was, they had stolen the dried grapes that I had bought and filled themselves up with them, so they were paying for their tricks, and I let them yell. The mother asked me to help them.

I said:

"If I do it will be with a horsewhip."

I was sick of them. In two days after this we came to Nevada, a town called Bunkesville, but they were all Mormons and Indians, painted up, and nearly baked.

We were sitting by a camp-fire one evening at dusk and several of the men had come to our camp to see us, when a tall, lanky old man came, and when he sat on a log by the fire one of the young men said:

"Well, Uncle Jonathan, you have gotten back. How many did you find on this trip?"

He was whittling a stick and had a plug of tobacco in his mouth, and a more repulsive looking thing in the shape of a man could not be found, and he drawled out:

"Well, I found sixty-two on this round up."

"And which did you like the best?"

"Well, I liked Martha the best. She had a

nice starched shirt all ready for me and nicer things to eat than any of the other wives."

Well, that did stagger me, for I thought that they had been rounding up cattle, but he had been going the rounds of his wives and had gotten sixty-two children, and, just like a beast, the one who fed him the best was his favorite. The squaws came around our wagon and stole everything they could get hold of. At night Luey, the ranchman, slept in one of the wagons, and in the night he heard someone in the wagon trying to steal some of our provisions. He got out in a hurry and grabbed his rifle, when something fell on his head and he thought it was a squaw's ear he got hold of, for he cried out:

"I have got her."

We were all up by this time. I went to Luey and said:

"What is the matter?"

He was holding a bedquilt and thought he was holding a squaw by the hair of the head, and when we began to look for the trouble we found two starving cats had gotten the meat and were chewing it as fast as they could, and they had made the noise and the quilt had fell on Luey's head, and in his excitement he thought he had hold of a squaw. He killed both the cats in a hurry before he knew what he was doing. Then I burst out laughing, for a more ridiculous sight could not be seen. A rifle in one hand and a corner of a bedquilt in the other, and his hair standing up with fright. He was yelling:

Captain Jack After a Day's Work.

"I have got her. I have got her."

We started the next day towards the Mohava Desert and filled everything with water that we could. We had a hard time, and when we had been on the desert two days and nights the water gave out and the horses suffered dreadfully, and the third day a wagon came along with two large barrels of water but they would not sell us any. I saw that we would lose our horses if they did not get water, so I took a five-dollar gold piece and said:

"Give the horses a drink and fill these jars and I will give you this. You will not want all that water, for you have broad tires and can get over in less time than it takes us."

This was more than they could let go, so they gave us half a barrel of water for the $5, and I was glad to pay it. The boys nearly killed themselves drinking, and at night of the third day we got to a farmyard near our camping grounds for the night.

We were in God's country again, with feed and water. We stayed that night and then got started the ensuing day and kept going for two days. Then we came to the Colorado river, which divides Nevada and Arizona. We could not cross this river except by ferry-boats. One of our wagon wheels had given out and we could not get any farther till new tires were sent. That was not all; the money was nearly all gone. We found out that over the Wallapys Desert there was a very good mining camp called the White Mills, and the deserts were fifty miles across, so I said to the women with boys:

"You had better go with the men and one wagon to the White Hills and then you will have to take care of yourself, for you have done nothing but eat and make work for me. I had to make all the bread. I had to go on my knees at night and make a wash boiler of bread and bake it before we started and you were not the women to offer to do anything, even wash the dishes, till you were called to help with them. Now, you go your way. I want no more of you."

So the next day one wagon with the men and the woman and three boys were towed over the Colorado river and went to the White Hills. I, with one wagon, was left alone. We had pitched our tent in a lane near the farmhouse. The people were Mormons, the women English and the men Swedes. They only had one wife, as they owned the ferry-boats and were well-to-do.

I waited three days, thinking that I would hear from the hills. but not a word came for me from the rest of the people, and on the fourth day the women came to me and said:

"We are going to an Indian funeral. You had better come with us. The wagon will be ready in half an hour.

I said:

"All right."

I was glad to get away somewhere, for I was getting worried about the other wagon and the people, so when they drove up to my camp I was ready and we started. We got there about 11:30 A. M., and there were swarms of Indians from far and near, and we got out of the wagons and walked to where the big crowd was, and there was a big, hot fire like a furnace and a pile of the hard redwood that grows there. We had not been there long when the most dismal howl and noise came—such a noise and such a crowd! It was deafening and awful, and to my horror they brought the man in the red blankets and put him on top of the hot fire and threw the logs on the top of him; then the others began to form a circle all around him on the top of the fire and howl and keep going around in a circle, and first one squaw and then another would jump to the fire and throw on some piece of her dress or apron that she had on. Then she brought the pony, but they had taken his hams and loins off him to have a feast of it at sundown, but the hide was there and they put it on the fire to burn with the man. I noticed one squaw was tearing all her clothes off and burning them, and I found out she was the wife of the buck, and she kept on burning until she found she had not a rag left on her, and the dismal noise and the smell and their throwing up of legs and arms in their dance around the fire was beyond description. No madhouse could compare with it, and at about twelve o'clock at night and at twelve at noon they all got under a bush and cried all through the moon. They called it crying, but it was howling, and it does not matter what they are doing, they stop and run under different bushes; a group under one bush and another under another bush, and one howls against the other, and beat their tom-toms, till it is deafening.

I waited ten days and no word came from the

rest of the party. Then I got a horse and as I had my side saddle with me I started for the White Hills over the desert. The people who owned the ferry were very much frightened at my going alone, but I laughed at them. They had good security for the horse, for I had left the wagon loaded with valuables. They towed me over the Colorado river and then landed me and left me to my fate.

I followed the road, but there was nothing but all kinds of cactuses and sand. I kept on until it was late, not a soul or sign of anything living could I see, and the horse was so tired he could hardly move. I got off and led him. It was getting very dark, but I kept on till it was late at night, when I saw a light a long way to the left of the road. I went till I could see there were lights on the hills. Then I knew the lights were from the mines, so kept on till I saw a town of tents and one with a lamp outside. I went up to it and when I got there found that it was a saloon. I went in and asked the man where I could put my horse. A man who was in camp came and took him. I told him to see that he was fed and had water. Then I went with the man to a place they called a hotel. I told them who I was and who I was looking for, and the next day I found the men. Frank had gone to work in the mines and Luey was working the horses, hauling asphalt for the corrals.

We got another tent and the cook stove was in the first wagon, so we went housekeeping, and the second night I was in camp there was a serenade, and they played the banjo and violin and sang beautifully. I did not know it was for me until the men said:

"Captain, get up; for they are serenading you."

I got up and dressed in a hurry. Then a crowd of men shouted:

"Welcome, Captain Jack, Queen of the Rockies."

Then the darkies began to play and sing:

"You are welcome to our shores."

The next morning I found out there were quite a number of Colorado boys and miners and prospectors working in the mines, and they knew I had come in camp. Some colored minstrels from California came to play in the gambling house, and they got them to come and serenade me. I thought I was where no one knew me and was surprised the next day. Some of the boys came and asked me if I had a hymn book or a prayer book, as two of the men were going to be buried, and if I would go and sing a hymn over them, so they that could be buried like men. They had built a hospital, two rooms for the sick, and they had a doctor. The men were dying every day, as the doctor said it was pneumonia.

I went to the funeral and sang two hymns, and all the men joined in, and as we were going home one of the head men of the company came to me and said:

"I wish you would go and see the sick men in the hospital and tell me what you think of them, for two of my foremen are there."

I went and looked at the men, four in all, and I knew they had not got pneumonia.

It was arsenic poison. The pupils of their eyes were closed and the color of their faces were yellow. They were all doomed for death. I told Mr. T. and he said:

"We will lose half of our men."

I said:

"Send and get a lot of sponges and elastic and dip the sponges in water and keep it over their mouths and nostrils. That will stop death, and the only thing that will kill the poison is greasy bacon and boiled milk, and as we are on a desert there is no milk."

The four men died that night and Mr. T. got the sponges and it stopped the poisoning. Two weeks after this I went with Luey and two of the horses on the desert to look at a place, where we picked up some fine looking rock. We started early, but it was farther than we thought. It was dark and we were a long way from home.

We came to a place where some one had been camping and had cut some wood, so we stopped to rest our horses and build a fire. We only had lunch with us, so had nothing for supper, but I took the newspaper that our lunch had been in and spread it on the ground to sleep on, saying to Luey:

"I have often joshed the boys that I could sleep under a bush if I had only a newspaper to sleep on, so here goes it. You watch the horses and the fire, for I am worn out."

I had not been to sleep when something was rattling the paper. It was getting up under my arm; it woke me up and I raised my head to see if it was Luey playing a trick on me, but there

Mrs. Captain Jack Lost in the Mountains.

he sat at the other side of the fire as he was when I lay down. Then something was right under the pit of my arm. I turned to see and to my horror there was a large rattlesnake.

I let a scream and rolled down the hill and the snake went up amongst the bushes. Luey yelled out:

"The darn thing is ten feet long."

The thing had gotten his head under my arm to get warm, and why it did not bite me was a wonder.

I said:

"Get the horses and we will work, for I want no more bedfellows like that." It was nearly morning when we got home, and I did not stop to undress, only loosen my clothes and it was late when I woke the next morning. The Indian chief was at the tent. He was a great, big man, over two hundred pounds, and he had a little girl's hat stuck on the top of his head. The hat was broad at the bottom and narrow at the top and had a dirty red ribbon around it. He looked like what we used to call a tomfool or a clown, when I first went in camp.

I made friends with him and gave him some paint and tobacco. It was a strange sight to see the tribe every Sunday sit in a circle on the ground, with stacks of silver dollars and three or four decks of cards and gamble, and the squaw would be standing up by their braves watching them like hawks, and if one of them lost all—his squaw would give him the last cent she had.

I had three jewsharps with me for which I had paid 25 cents apiece. The Indians offered me $5 for one, so I sold it to them. They came for the other two at the same price. They would lend it for a few minutes and then the other squaws would try to play it, but they had no tune but the dreadful howling.

A few days after this one of our boys bought two monsters in a cage with iron bars on. He bought them for male and female. They would close their eyes, swell their necks, then throw their poison out like a pale green stream, and it was sure death to get it on man or beast. The third day they got in a fight and they set up on their hind legs and fought till one got the other by the throat and killed it. They were both males. There is nothing on earth that is worse than they are. The man paid $9 for a case of eggs to feed them. I took my gun and shot the other, for I would not have the monster near the tent.

I found out that the rich mine, the "Grand Army," was bought from one of the Indians for a plug of tobacco and a half pint of whisky. The mine paid millions. "Them," the chief, came to see me every day. He told me that there was an old Mormon fort at the mouth of Death Valley and under the floor there was a heap of gold hidden. He said that he would take me to it, but the boys said it was not safe for me to go if he would not let them go too. We all would go. We paid $1.50 per barrel for water. It had to be hauled nine miles from what they called a water hole. It was warm and nasty. How I longed for one good drink of that Colorado clear water, and as I sat all alone on that clear moonlight night, thinking of the cause of this dry desert, I could but think there is another triangle, and its law is repulsion, retention, suppression and attraction, for what holds large quantities of water and snow which falls to earth. There is nothing neutral, and it attracts from earth and is retained in the clouds until the right attraction draws it down That same law is attached to everyone of us; some repulse and others attract; some keep friends and others' friends are of short duration, and it is plain to understand that these forces all work by triangle power.

A few weeks after this there was a stir in camp. Groups of Indians were getting together with looks of anger on their faces, and crowds of white men were talking together, when to my surprise they came toward my tents. I went to the door to meet them, when the proprietor of the big gambling house came and said:

"Captain, we want you to help us out of a messy scrap. The man who owned the largest corral in town got full last night and dragged a squaw in his office and abused her. The Indians will do mischief if something is not done. We are going to arrest Jake and then turn my gambling room into a courtroom and try him, and we want you to be the judge, for Tom, the chief, will stand by you where he does not trust one of us."

I said:

"Well, you are getting me in a strange business; first, you make a minister of me to read the funeral services and sing, and now you want me to be a judge, which I do not want to be. Let the men take care of the case."

"That is what we are going to do, but the chief is so angry that we fear bloodshed, and if we can avoid it by being cautious it is the best thing to save life and property, for the chief is one of the worst brutes and fighters of all the tribes. He saw you shoot the monster the other day and said:

" 'The Paleface heap brave and shoot good,' and he slapped his breast in admiration of you.

"Now we know it is not a nice thing to ask you to do, but you have the sand and sense and are gritty. You know you fear nothing, and if you are the judge the chief will not let the braves turn loose on us, for we want you to come and help us out, for we must do what we are going to do quick, before they get started to burn the town and butcher our people, for it is known that there are no troops nearer than Frisco."

I said:

"Go ahead and get your man."

So they got a roll of rope and bound his arms with it and took him up to the courtroom. It was soon packed with miners and Indians.

Then they sent for the squaw and her husband and the chief. Then I went in and played judge.

I asked her to tell what he did. She opened her shawl and showed me the bruises on her arms and wounds on her breast where he had bitten her like a brute.

I asked her to show me the man. She showed me the prisoner. I asked the man why he did it. He said that he was drunk and did not know what he was doing. Then the chief said:

"If my braves did that to the Paleface, you would hang him and make war with the rest of them."

I said:

"Well, I will fine you $50 and costs and you will pay the $50 to the squaw before you leave this room."

Then I beckoned to the squaw to come to me. The man said he did not have that much money, and that he only had $30. He put the $30 on the table. I got the men to give me silver for it, then told him he must borrow the rest. I knew that the chief was watching every move that I made. Then some of the men said:

"Let us all chip in."

So they took up a collection. I counted $20 more of silver dollars and gave it to the squaw, saying:

"This will make it all right. I made him pay for his drunkenness and cruelty."

The hard, cruel look passed from the chief's face and changed to a smile. He whipped out a large sharp dagger and held it up and said:

"I come here to put it in his breast. But the Paleface has done better, and the next Paleface that is bad to my squaws I will kill him."

I said:

"Yes, but you will not let your braves do anything of harm, now I have settled this?"

He said:

"Give me your hand. I will see not anyone is hurt. You have done well."

Then I counted the balance of the money and had $42 left.

I said:

"Let this money start a burial fund, for so many of the boys that die have no money and are so far away from home and friends, and every pay day throw in a mite. It will grow and he that ate poison will be pleased to know you will not be buried a pauper."

They all shouted and got excited. I thought they were crazy, and I was afraid and thought they would get into a fight, for they had been so still through it all, but none did, and now all was settled.

They gave vent to their feelings and yelled like madmen, and when I got up to go they picked me up and put me on their shoulders and carried me to my tent.

It was not many days after this that it was a warm night. I felt something in my bed. I could not sleep, and as soon as daylight came I got up to see what it was in the bed, and to my horror there was a swarm of lizards; the Indians called them "swifts." They ran up and down the walls of the tent in swarms. That settled it. I would not stay in such a place, so I began to get ready to leave for Colorado. When night came I went to the only building called a hotel to sleep, for I was afraid of these lizards.

It was a clear moonlight night the anniversary of the 27th year I had been in the West, and the stage was to leave the next morning at five o'clock for Kingman and take me with it. I had been talking to the Indians about their form of worship, and when I stood at my tent door I could not help wandering away for quite a distance on the desert. The large cactuses seemed to take different forms. They called them "Joshuas" there. In the moonlight they looked like men and animals. I had gone out of sight of the town of tents, when I sat on a fallen "Joshua" and sat musing with my thoughts, and my mind flew backwards to that old thatched-roof house where we had a Bible over five hundred years old, and in one place it said:

"If your wife offend thee, scourge her with a whip."

But woman's intelligence soon came to their aid and they would not let their children go to church or school to be taught such things, and when the priests tried to frighten them to send their children and go themselves they stood firm and said:

"No, we will call on God to save us from the sting of the lash when our husband is inflicting it on us and our conscience tells us that God never made man so big and strong to use that strength on the weaker women with a whip, and we shall not have our children taught to do such things or our girls to submit to being whipped by their husbands."

So they had to cut out of the Bible that part and stop preaching it or have the churches all to themselves. So women, with the God-given weaker body, had the power to defy the cunning

14

priestcraft and civilize the brute man. Let us go further. They get up a hell fire and brimstone and tell the people if they do not go to church and believe what is told them, or do anything contrary to its teaching, this Almighty God will burn them forever, so stay in your flight through life and take a few minutes to analyze this and see what blasphemy this is. This was frightful. The people blaspheme the all-wise God, but build up your churches is the cry of all creeds. There is a creed in India where the women throw their infants in the river and watch the alligators eat them up as a sacrifice to this hungry God. Intelligence comes in and stops this, but our churches of today are far worse than the alligator creed, for the women did not make the alligator eat their young, but all creeds admit that God made man; then, according to the creed of today, he made man to be murdered; for when he made man he knew what man would do and how long it would take to bring him to the light of reason and intelligence. Yet they set up another God born from animal woman whom they call Christ and claim him to be the only son of God, and worship him, but they forget that if God had a son he must have had a mother the same as his father in spirit; but creed says that God the Father, Son and Holy Ghost, leaving out the mother as nothing and putting the Holy Ghost in her place; then they get together and murder him in the most cruel form, then tell the people he died to save them all from—what? Was it from the anger of this fatherly loving God who made man the two-legged alligator to murder his only son as a sacrifice to be murdered by man that he created himself? They ought to know that God is a spirit, and if he has a son, that son would come in his astral body, in the brightest sunlight or in the darkest night, and he would see and hear in every language, but no man would lay hands on Him, for they that tried would fall dead from the electricity from his body before they could get near enough to touch Him.

The Buddhists claim to have the only one, the Chaldeans claim to have the only one, and the Mohammedans claim to have the only one, and so it has been for ages back.

The Indian, who knows no teacher, goes out at sunrise in the morning and worships the big spirit which his higher self teaches him is right, for what is man and what is soul? The body of man is the casing of the spiritual body and the spiritual body is the casing of the soul and indestructible. When a child is born there is no life till the breath enters that body with the spiritual body, and when it dies the breath, with the spiritual body, the germ of the God which is the soul, all leaves that human body as the workings of a clock taken from its case, and yet creed will try to save their souls. There is no such thing as a soul. There is no such thing as a soul being lost. You cannot lose your soul or destroy it. Better pray for light and wisdom. As I have said before, there are three powers that control all things—electricity, vibration, and what I called the Push is an aura light that is around every living thing and controls every creature, and works with planetary vibrations, according to the position of the planets. The God head essence is in this light; if we could only understand their harmony and working together we would all be a better race of people.

And after twenty-seven years of wandering through the Rocky Mountains in the far West I drop amongst the people as though I came from the clouds, and what do I find: That our public schools are teaching both boys and girls to be sports. The girls feel degraded to go out and do housework, and they know nothing of sewing and housekeeping, and want a piano the first thing. The boys will not work and are looking for a soft snap, to be a doctor or lawyer or a politician—anything to get a graft out of the public—and the brainy men that are fitted for these positions are at their wit's end to know how to compete with this army of grafters; and as I wander on I find a lot of people banded together as temperance unions, or different names, who have been reformed drunkards and had to take a big oath and have a mob at their backs to keep them from getting drunk. These are all degenerates, for if man or woman cannot drink beer, wine or liquor without getting beastly intoxicated, he has no will power and is a degenerate. These people are a curse to the country, for they say, "We do not drink now and you shall not drink." So they want to take the rights of the level-headed people away, who do not say we drink and you must let these people go back to olden times. When we had good mothers they taught their children to drink without being drunkards, as they taught them to eat without being gluttons. Mothers, stay at home and teach your children to eat, drink and work and be good men and women, instead of drunkards, degenerates and drones; even the bees know enough to destroy their drones.

I look farther and I find they have built railroads under rivers in New York and built buildings twenty and thirty stories high. In every city where there are large sheets of water there is a liability of a volcanic eruption which they call earthquake. When they come, I would rather be in the mountains than near those high buildings.

And as I look farther I find in all large cities they are persecuting the Jews. They will not admit them in the hotels and will not rent them houses in certain parts of the cities. Hark, all ye Hebrews; hear the prophecy of the Fairy who wears a crown of silvery gray; hear, now, the time is fast coming when this persecution shall cease, for you are the coming people of this nation; you are the commercial people of this country; now you are in the light of progression whilst two-thirds of our people are degenerates, and in time to come this mighty nation shall be the Promised Land of the Jews.

So, cheer up, for the aura light is breaking through the dark circle of apprehension.

And this is the prophecy of the Fated Fairy and a wanderer for twenty-seven years in the far West.

Breinigsville, PA USA
15 March 2011
257696BV00003B/1/P